STIMULI

STIMULI

by

R. A. KNOX

SHEED AND WARD
LONDON AND NEW YORK

FIRST PUBLISHED 1951
BY SHEED AND WARD, LTD.
110/111 FLEET STREET,
LONDON, E.C.4
AND
SHEED AND WARD, INC.
830 BROADWAY,
NEW YORK, 3

To K

PRINTED IN GREAT BRITAIN
BY PURNELL AND SONS, LTD.
PAULTON (SOMERSET) AND LONDON

PREFACE

"SHARP goads they are to sting us, these words of the wise"; the claim can be made, not for one book of Scripture but for the whole of Scripture, and indeed for the writings of the spiritual authors in every age. Beware of such reading, if your aim is to pass through life in a haze of comfortable mediocrity; hidden under the surface, these books contain barbs here and there, ready to pierce the skin of your conscience, though it be as tough to kick the goad as the university of Tarsus can make it. You are never safe from this disagreeable sensation of pricking, just where you thought you were case-hardened. Only—it has to be admitted—the edge of these salutary weapons is blunted for us by familiarity; we have read the same consecrated formulae of words so often that we have learned how to skate over them, without letting them make any impact on the mind. That is why they need refurbishing; they must be stated in other words, their uncomfortable implications must be brought out, thrown into relief. That, and nothing else, is the true office of the preacher. When the Roman poet resigns himself to do a whetstone's work, that sharpens though it does not know how to cut, he is a model for us all; if we draw blood, it is with no point of ours.

It has been the custom to leave the man at the whetstone plenty of elbow room; and even in these more strenuous days we do not find fault with a sermon if it is the right side of twenty minutes. The sermons (if they can be called sermons) of which this book is composed are still more severely rationed, and leave little space for the grinding process. The reason is, they were first published in the *Sunday Times*, where space is hard to come by, and although it would have been easy to distend them, they have been left in their original form. They may catch the eye, now and again, of somebody who would protest that he was too busy to read a whole sermon. And a gnat's sting is better than no sting at all.

Have I written as though the book consisted of nothing but scoldings? I would not have it thought so. Many of these lightning meditations (if I may give them that name) were written during the War, when one's friends seemed to need comfort rather than admonition. We still need comfort, and may yet need it more: let us have the oil and wine of the Samaritan.

CONTENTS

I

ROUND THE YEAR

CONTENTS

II

A Few Saints

III

This and That

CONTENTS

I
ROUND THE YEAR

I

THE DATED RELIGION

I HOPE I am not alone in feeling a peculiar thrill when I read, or hear read, the beginning of the gospel on the fourth Sunday of Advent, " In the fifteenth year of the emperor Tiberius's reign "—and then the long list of the local rajahs. It feels like a gun going off; a maroon, rather, for it is at once sudden and staccato. A catastrophic reminder that something of infinite importance took place at a finite moment in time.

Actually, it is a false alarm. What is specifically recorded is not the appearance of a Redeemer, but the emergence from obscurity of John the Baptist, some 30 years later. And, indeed, few events can be dated with so little precision as the true Christian era : Quirinius has seen to that. Nevertheless, it is dated : Quirinius's register, whenever it happened, issued an identity card to a Divine Person. Eternity, instead of remaining in the background, swam for one moment into the orbit of time, and challenged our sublunary attention.

That, I suppose, is the meaning of Advent, that is why we force our time-conditioned minds, once a year, into an artificial mood of expectancy. We are children, if you like, playing a game of make-believe; let's pretend, for four weeks, that the world is still unredeemed, so that at the end of it we may have the thrill of saying, " I told you so ; he's come! " We will have a zero-hour, at which for once Mass shall be celebrated at what is nominally the same time all the world over. To celebrate the birth of Christ at a moment when it is not happening is to remind

3

ourselves, *ex hypothesi*, that there was a moment when it did.

To be sure we date ourselves ; we belong to a religion which is bound up with something which happened a great many years ago. And, to our generation, there is a mysterious reproach about being "dated"; you are not of the 1951 vintage, therefore you do not count. I suppose there is nothing which so dates our generation as this habit of talking about things being dated. In proportion as you succumb to the habit, you make a fool of yourself by assuming that 1951 is the measure of all time and existence; that what we think is of course right, and what those other people thought was of course wrong.

Not to celebrate Christmas Day is to have only one birthday in the year ; is to have no *point d'appui* for your thought outside yourself. You get away from the treadmill of your own thought when you learn to wish the world, annually, many happy returns of its Redemption.

II

SOME OTHER

" IS IT *thy* coming that was foretold, or are we yet
waiting for some other ? " Each year, St. John the
Baptist's question awakes a cowardly echo in our
hearts—What if, after all, the decisive revelation
should be something still unrevealed ? Prophets and kings
desired it long, and died before the sight ; but this advantage
they had over us, they could picture the advent of the
Messias in terms of rosy anticipation, as accompanied by
an earthly millennium which has never (as we of a later
time know) materialised. Amazing signs, yes, accompanied
and accredited that first-century advent ; but this was not
all Isaias prophesied. The lion and the lamb fraternising,
has there been any sign of it, then or since ?

For us, who have learned to put a Christian construction
on the sum of our experience, the doubt remains a scruple
only. We hail the first Advent as seed-time, not harvest ;
grain must grow secretly, tares mingled with it ; the
leaven must have time to work. The dream of the schismatic
Franciscans, that we might expect a third, post-Christian
dispensation, that of the Holy Spirit, has a recurrent
attraction for visionary minds, but cannot be squared with
any kind of traditional orthodoxy.

What, though, of those others, never (or never effectively)
seized of the Christian inheritance, who, like St. John,
are " scandalised "—complain that the Advent we preach
is not the Advent they bargained for ? Perhaps we can
afford to be a little tender with their hesitations. Granted
(they say) that the dawn which came at Bethlehem was

5

that of a splendid Ideal, may we not, after all these centuries, strain our eyes towards some new dawn, of a religion which will be really operative in the development of human history?

The answer is an ungracious one, but it must be made nevertheless. It is, that the dawn which came at Bethlehem, whether they are satisfied with it or not, is all the dawn they are going to get. (I mean, so far as religion is concerned; let him comfort himself who will with the Utopias of the materialist.) That the Christian revelation is the last supernatural revelation the world can expect, is the verdict not only of theology, but of experience. Bethlehem has exhausted the world's capacity for worship. Only one great religion has arisen since; a palpable throw-back to the Old Testament. All our other adventures have been variations of the Christian theme; the dead gods do not rise. What Bethlehem has given us is an austerity religion; it never pretended to be anything else. The Christian religion has been the great romance of the human heart, which is staled now for all other loves, and un-regretfully.

III

THE ROD OF JESSE

ONE OF the old antiphons for the days just before Christmas refers to the prophecy made by Isaias, " There shall come forth a rod out of the root of Jesse, and a flower shall rise up out of his root." The Fathers, for the most part, identify the Flower with our Lord Jesus Christ, the Rod with his Blessed Mother, from whom he takes his kinship with earth. We are to think of a root which has already given birth to a great tree, that has grown old now, gnarled and withered with age. In defiance of our expectations, it has power to put forth shoots once more. From the base of that knotted trunk springs a single branch, and from that branch the flower which is its perfection.

The root of Jesse, the old dynasty of Judah, has little meaning for us now. The wicked Ahab, the devout Josias, what ripple have they left on the surface of history ? They fought and intrigued and took their pleasures,

> *Till in due time, one by one,*
> *Some with lives that came to nothing, some with deeds as*
> *   well undone,*
> *Death stepped tacitly and took them where they never see*
> *   the sun.*

Jesse, and David, the son of Jesse, mean no more to us than other great memories in the lumber-room of the past. But because from that stock our Lord's Mother and our Lord himself came to us, they are not forgotten. Their root

7

lingers in grateful remembrance, through that divine after-thought which its failing energies produced.

In a world of great sinfulness that genealogy heralds the restoration of man's innocence. Man's winter, God's spring : the living branch growing from the dead root ; for that, year by year, we Christians give thanks when Advent comes round. It is something that has happened once for all ; we look for no further revelation, no fresh redemption. Yet there are times in history when the same mood of despair comes upon us in which the world, Jewish and pagan, was sunk at the time when Jesus Christ was born. Old landmarks seem obliterated, and the old certainties by which we lived seem to have deserted us ; the world seems to have exhausted itself, and has no vigour left to face its future. The world's winter, God's spring ; he never fails to make his power known in fresh miracles of fecundity.

We are so engrossed in our own plans, five years' plans and ten years' plans, and the rest of it, that we assume they must be God's plans too. We have grown so accustomed to our familiar certainties, that when a shock is felt which makes these seeming-solid foundations of ours tremble, we go about crying that the end of the world has come. But for all we can tell, God may be working out a five thousand years' plan or a ten thousand years' plan of his own ; we may still be living, for all we know, in the early Church.

IV

MAKE-DO AND MAKE-BELIEVE

CHRISTMAS is the season of make-believe; we all associate it with stockings that turn into cornucopias, with paper crowns, with trees whose fruit is glittering glass and tinsel. As you find yourself building up the Christmas Crib with brown paper to look like rocks and salts from the chemist to look like snow, you are haunted by a slight sense of guilt; is not such make-believe an irreverence, when it is associated with religion? But you can comfort yourself with the reflection that after all make-believe is only make-do. Lacking the facilities for making a real cave, we make the best sort of cave we can, as long as even brown paper is forthcoming. War-time has left us well accustomed to the *ersatz*.

And, indeed the anniversary we celebrate is itself an occasion of make-believe and make-do. The picture we have to conjure up is that of two Jewish evacuees, unbefriended in a strange town with a third Life to provide for in addition to their own. The quality we acclaim in them is that splendid kind of humility which always makes the best of what is to be had; which cries out, "A stable? The very thing! A manger? Why, it looks as if it had been meant for a cradle!" The immediate practical lesson of Christmas is surely, in war-time at least, the lesson of cheerfulness in cramped conditions. There is a real humility in imitating a God who was born in a utility nursery, and laid in an austerity cradle to match it.

This earthly humility is after all only the reflection, only the human coefficient, of that Divine Humility which planned and executed the whole mystery of Christmas Day. If God would become Man the whole human life he chooses must necessarily be a life of make-do. If he had been born in a palace that palace would have been hopelessly inadequate to the situation. If his own had received him the reception would have been well-meaning enough, but how *gauche*, how tentative! The whole activity of the Incarnation meant a kind of make-do ; a Divine Personality cramped in his self-expression, even when he had a perfect Humanity to express himself in. You might almost say, it was a kind of make-believe ; not in the sense that he did not really become Man, but in the sense that humanity at best is, by comparison, a sort of shadow-substance ; indequate to be the tenement of such a Guest.

Yet how make *us* believe, if he did not talk our own language ? How make *us* do, if he did not accept our limitations and plan out for us the perfect human life ?

V

THE WORLD-SOLSTICE

PEOPLE who want to know why Christmas is kept on December 25 are told, " Oh, because of the Saturnalia." But what had Saturn to do with it ? And the Saturnalia began on the 17th. No, the old ceremonies of the Saturnalia were transferred ; the feast of misrule to December 6, the present to December 25—that is all. If a reason is wanted, it was surely because of the solstice. The winter solstice is a kind of annual mercy ; just as high tide saves us from a repetition of the flood, the shortest day saves us from a repetition of the Egyptian darkness. Fitting, evidently, that the Dayspring from on high should visit us just then.

The winter solstice is the year's bottle-neck, reminding you of that dreadful moment when a football-match crowd has to squeeze through the gate. It is the acme of our winter discontent ; things have had to get worse (as the politicians say) before they can get better. Hence our instinct of beginning the New Year not, like the old Romans, in lambing-time, but a week after the solstice, when we have made sure that the days are really drawing out. To us Christians, the first Christmas Day is the solstice or bottle-neck of history. Things got worse till then, ever since we had lost Paradise ; things are to get better since then, till we reach Paradise once more. History is shaped like an X.

That conception, I admit, is based on theology rather than on experience. You cannot prove that things were getting worse and worse till the year A.D. 0, or whatever it was. But I think you can say the world was becoming more conscious of its badness, anyhow, up till the time of Virgil's Messianic eclogue, and the date fixed by Daniel; there was a growing demand for deliverance. Then deliverance came; not felt all at once (Juvenal and the Apocalypse tell you that), but then, the solstice is felt, at first, only at one end. Nor can you prove that things have been getting better and better since A.D. 0. Indeed, times such as our own, like a snowy day in March, make you wonder whether things have got better at all. But cheerfulness will keep on coming in: you feel sure that the main impetus is towards the good ever since those days of the amphitheatre. It is only the perennial weakness of human nature which produces a side-slip in the machine, such as we are experiencing to-day.

If you doubt that, recall your own good resolutions of last New Year. How many side-slips about *them*? If the individual can show no record of unchequered progress, it ill becomes him to blame his world of fellow-individuals for showing, now and again, a corporate relapse. But take courage, Christmas will reassert itself; the world is not going to find itself celebrating the Odinalia. Let your own good resolutions, already three days old, be the pledge of that.

VI

RENEWAL

THE difference between the Old and the New
Testaments is the difference between a man who
said " There is nothing new under the sun " and
a God who says " Behold, I make all things new."
It is the measure of the extent to which circumstances
have got us down, that we have not been wishing one
another, this first of January, a happy new year *sans phrase*.
We have found ourselves modestly hoping that the new
year will not treat our friends too hardly, jocosely wishing
that they may find something to be happy about. Our
prophets have been at a loss to imagine any kind of future
which the public will enjoy when it comes.

Happiness, however you define it, depends on harmonis-
ing with your environment. And if we find it so difficult to
make our environment harmonise with our own tastes,
I hope it is no very craven counsel to suggest that we should
set about it the other way. I mean, that we should wish one
another, not so much surroundings more congenial to our
temper, as a temper more congenial to our surroundings.

I hasten to add that I am speaking of a supernatural, not
a natural change. To be conditioned by your surroundings
merely in the sense that you have got accustomed to them
is the very thing we are all trying to avoid—slavery. It
is something quite different, when St. Paul hopes that the
Ephesians will experience a renewal in the inner life of their
minds. He is wishing for them, not a subservience which
will bow to destiny, but a resilience which will challenge
destiny to do its worst.

13

STIMULI

It is one of the most unfortunate mistranslations of his thought when he is represented as saying that God will provide with the "temptation" (that is, the trial of our constancy) a "way of escape." No, God will ordain the issue; and at the same time he will enable us to hold our own. Our natural instinct when we have travelled through a dark patch of history, is to talk about the end of the tunnel. Our past endurance (that is how we picture it) gives us the right to expect better times. Supernaturally, the moral we ought to draw is surely that if God enabled us to stand up to yesterday, he can fortify us against the most disagreeable of tomorrows.

VII

STAR OF BETHLEHEM

IF WE were strict in our interpretation of it, only Jews would celebrate Christmas Day. Shepherd folk, plying the trade of the twelve patriarchs and of King David, received an angelic message which promised peace (that is, security) to men God loved (that is, to Israel), tidings to them, and to all the (Chosen) People; " to all people " is an inexcusable mistranslation. The Saviour, the Christ to whose coming they looked forward, was to be a national Saviour, a Davidic Ruler. They asked for no more.

Epiphany, that follows so confusingly on the heels of Christmas, is really a celebration of the same event. But God forbid that we should regard it as a distinction without a difference; this is where we poor miserable Gentiles come in. The word means what our ancestors called a manifestation, and we call a show-down.

Heaven, for once, shows its hand : the Divine purpose that is at work all the time behind the scenes of history gives itself away, as if by a faulty stage effect, and the light of eternity shines through. It is used, sometimes, of our Lord's Second Coming, sometimes of his First ; in the second chapter of Titus you will find it applied to both. But it is in the first chapter of Second Timothy that you must look for the *locus classicus* : " It was not because of anything we had done ; we owe it to his own design. ... Now it has come to light, since our Saviour Jesus Christ came to enlighten us." Not because of anything we had done, sacrifice offered or sabbath kept ; it was for us Gentiles too. The glorious gift

15

of salvation made at Bethlehem proved, when the wrappings
of it were unwound, more glorious than we had dared to
hope. We scanned the stars in search of omens and such-
like fooleries ; and for once a real message came through.

That mystery which St. Paul revealed, that message
which St. Paul preached, the emancipation of the Gentiles,
has lost something of its thrill for us. We take it for granted
now, that the Gospel is meant for all mankind; obviously,
why shouldn't it be ? And, as is the way with men who take
things for granted, we forget to pinch ourselves and go on
asserting it.

Even in our own lives, how fond we are of making a
little enclave, a little Bethlehem that just has head-room
for our set, and leaving the rest of the world unshepherded!
But Epiphany signals to us that all men have rights, have
duties, are dear to Christ. We have seen his Star, and our
sympathies must be no narrower than his Planet.

VIII

THE INTRUSION OF THE WISE MEN

MOST of us feel that Epiphany is something of an anti-climax after Christmas. The Crib, as we saw it on Christmas morning, had such an air of intimacy and domesticity about it. " There were *in the same country* shepherds "—it was only the immediate neighbours that had been called in; there was no general publicity. The appearance of black men and camels at the doorway enriches the scene only at the expense of making it less friendly ; we have lost the sense that the lodge was tiled, the sense of a family party. So, belief in a world religion reduces the sense of cosiness, of neighbourliness, which makes the atmosphere of a small sect agreeable to our natural prejudices. We lose our sense of individuality when we are called upon to think with the mind of Tom, Dick, and Harry.

But it is worse than that ; Tom, Dick, and Harry would not matter so much ; they are shepherd-folk like ourselves. These new visitors bring with them, not only the exotic airs of a strange country, but a whiff of intellectualism. What brought them here ? Not the direct assurance of a personal message given by an angel ; only a laborious inference from the mechanised movement of the uncompanionable stars. They are *wise* men, interrupting our Feast of Fools. " A Saviour, who is Christ the Lord "—that was the plain formula which had rallied us, sinners wanting a Saviour, not caring much about anything else. But these new voices outside are asking about a King ; we had heard nothing of that. A waft of incense-smoke overpowers the warm fragrance of the hay; it is more than a King, it is a God they are looking for. Myrrh is in their hands ; they are asking questions about life, death, and eternity. The Star that hangs over the Crib becomes a kind of asterisk, adding footnotes to our plain text.

So, if we would have a religion which is not only wide as the world, but broad as the compass of man's mind, a multitude of questions must be asked and answered. We can no longer rest content with one-syllable slogans like " Peace on earth to the men who are God's friends "; our religion must have an attitude towards vexed questions of world-politics, of the Absolute, of personal survival : the states-man, the philosopher, the scientist will call for a definition of what we stand for. There will always be a tendency, more marked in transitional times, for Christians to demand a faith free from the trammels of theology, the processes, star-led and camel-borne, of the human reason. But an un-intellectual salvation means an unsaved intellect. The Child grew in wisdom, as well as in stature.

IX

PIECRUST SUNDAY

THIS IS, I am afraid, a festival of my own invention unknown to liturgy. But many of us make good resolutions to usher in the New Year, and the observance of good resolutions, with most of us, lasts a full fortnight and no longer. Surely then, the third Sunday in January is an opportunity for cultivating that baffled spirit of humiliation which is, commonly, the only fruit our good resolutions bring.

Why is our performance so barren? No need to improve the occasion by reminding ourselves that we are fallen creatures. Adam was without that excuse, and Adam fell. No need to expatiate on our need of grace, grace is the supernatural co-efficient of human effort, not a substitute for it. Best take ourselves for what we are, and acknowledge that the spirit of self-seeking is rarely absent from our efforts at self-improvement, the spirit of injured vanity rarely absent from our confessions of failure.

Oddly enough, we seem to be more successful when our endeavours are purely self-regarding, have no relish of salvation in them. Much easier to find a man who has corrected his tendency to pull his drives than a man who has conquered the habit of uncharitable talk. Do we, perhaps, fall between two stools when we make our more important resolutions? Do we blindly set out to do something for God in a patronising spirit without trying to find out what it is he wants us to do, how and in what measure he wants us to do it?

I believe there are one or two rules worth observing. One is, to aim at something positive, not something negative.

Occasional and even frequent failures to keep a positive resolution do not bring with them the same chilling sense of despair. You are less likely to throw up the sponge after the fourth failure to rise when you are called than after the fourth row with your sister-in-law.

Another is to supplement—replace if you will—the habit of thinking up good resolutions at certain seasonable intervals by the habit of following up, at once, the good inspirations which come to us by flashes ; the good inspirations which tempt us to say, " That will do for Lent." Why wait till Lent to do something which might be done on January the twentieth?

A third is to pray for the grace to carry out the resolve, and to let your mind dwell on the prayer rather than on the resolve itself. Commonly, the man who thinks he is going to win does better than the man who tries hard to win.

But, above all, when you come back to report failure, let it be with a smile.

X

FROM THE EAST AND FROM THE WEST

WE THOUGHT we had finished with the Epiphany, but the Church, as if uncertain what to talk about next, has given us a gospel this Sunday which is an agreeable pendant to the story of the Wise Men. Those providential godfathers at our Lord's cradle, with their mystical avenue of approach, their mystical birth-day presents, seemed to represent an infiltration of Eastern thought into Christendom. Silently they make their salaams and disappear into the unknown countries whence they came. This is to be one of those Eastern religions, you feel—not much to do with real life.

And then to-day's Westerner comes in, to clear the incense-laden atmosphere with his Western, practical ways of thought. An N.C.O. of the Roman army, from any part of Europe—Britain, if you like—whose native boy has gone sick; can't something be done? The suggestion " I will come and heal him" takes this man by surprise; shocks him, almost. The proper place for the G.O.C. is at G.H.Q., not in the front line ; so here, our Lord has forces at his disposal, and if he bids them " Do this," it is done ; no need for him to come and make a tour of inspection. " My place isn't fit for you to visit, Sir ; a word of command will do." You can almost hear the click of his heels as he says it. This is the contribution the West will make to Christendom, " the Roman line, the Roman order " ; it will be a coherent body, officered, regimented ; there will be words of command.

STIMULI

Not only wise men from the East, then ; we fools from the West are in the picture, too. Our Lord draws an Epiphany moral ; " many shall come from the east and from the west "—he represents his kingdom as a family meal, with Abraham at the head of the table surrounded by a crowd of foreigners, while his own children (for how long ?) flatten their noses against a blacked-out window. The inn that was too proud is contrasted with the house that was too modest to entertain a heavenly Guest. " The children shall be cast out "—we are not meant to visit the Christmas crib entirely in a spirit of self-congratulation. Other people, who had (if we may say it without smugness) dimmer lights, lesser graces than our own, are so apt to out-strip us Church-abiding people in the very qualities that ought to come naturally from us; self-sacrifice on the heroic level, cheerfulness and kindliness in the common walks of life. " From the east and from the west " ; whose fault will it be if we find ourselves, one day, ruefully contemplating the door-scraper that has served those travel-stained feet ?

XI

THE ASH WEDNESDAY MESSAGE

IN THE traditional ceremonies of Ash Wednesday, the priest smears ashes on the foreheads of the congregation, saying as he does so, " Remember, Man, that thou art dust, and unto dust shalt thou return." It is not a specially religious sentiment, this. The heathen poets rub it in till we are tired of it, and the people who write angry books against religion are always repeating it to us savagely as if it were a point that had never occurred to us. Whereas if they had read the Book of Genesis they would have found it on the threshold of the Bible.

True, that is not the whole account of the matter. Alone among the creatures, man can look back upon himself and become the object of his own thought, can distinguish the world he knows from himself as knowing it. In the exercise of that faculty, he transcends the limits of mere matter. Nevertheless he is dust. The liaison between body and soul must not be explained away by talking as if the body were a cage which imprisons, or a garment which clothes, the soul. This body of mine is myself. And we are encouraged at the beginning of Lent, to humiliate ourselves by remembering what, on that side of our nature, we are.

The Ash Wednesday message is at the same time one of comfort. For, as the Psalm tells us, God " knows our fashioning; he remembers that we are but dust." We need to be reminded of it once a year; he remembers it all the time. He knows all the flaws in our make-up which predispose us to this or that bad habit; the force of every temptation. If we are tempted to lose heart because we so often fall short of our own ideals, are false to our own natures, it is important once again to remember that we are dust; there is a natural instability about us which explains, and perhaps extenuates, actions which it cannot excuse.

It is not plain dust that is used on Ash Wednesday, but ashes—those of the palms which were carried in procession on Palm Sunday the year before. It is the dead remains of something we can remember as a living thing not so very long ago; the embers of glory. The symbolism of that is plain and hackneyed enough.

The ashes are a foretaste of the dust that will rattle, one day, on our coffin. And, by a kind of grim irony, spring, early or late, is the moment chosen for this importunate reminder. Just when earth is beginning to put out its first shy promise of green, we are plucked by the sleeve and reminded that we are dust. Several of the Saints have owed their conversion to the contemplation of an open tomb. But the experience came to them in youth ; only so can it come as a revelation. I suppose that is why Lent happens in spring.

XII

FORTY DAYS' GRACE

WHEN Lent begins, your Minister of the gospel suddenly takes upon himself the character of an Ambassador. " God appeals to you through us ; we entreat you in Christ's name, make your peace with God." Christ is the victorious general, imposing terms on the rebels ; the preacher, acting as his deputy, implores the congregation not to give this offer of pardon an ineffectual welcome. " Here is the time of pardon," he adds ; and the laity, incurious as usual, forget to ask what time he is referring to.

The notion, surely, is that we are to treat the 40 days of Lent as a sacramental expression of something that is going on all the while. We are, all the while, being given a little more time to repent in, before God grows weary and cuts us off in our sins. The gardener is appealing to his master to spare the fig-tree one year longer ; one year of intensive cultivation, to give it a last chance. Odd, that in law we use the same term, " days of grace " : the bill is due already, but the debtor has three more days for payment. Did law get the phrase from theology? " Worldliness like yours," the preacher says, " would give God a perfectly good excuse for cutting you off, here and now, in your sins. What holds his hand is the appeal of Calvary. He is giving you a little more time to repent in; let us call it forty days. After that, if you remain impenitent, I cannot answer for what will happen."

Is the right recipe for Lent, then, to live as we would if we were certainly to die on Good Friday? No harm in the

idea, but it misses the point. God's threats are conditional;
when Jonah cried " Yet forty days, and Nineveh shall be
overthrown," he meant, not that the city was doomed in
any case, but that only repentance could save it. In these
days, when nations rather than individuals have become the
units of history, perhaps we should think of sin abandoned
as our one hope of staving off the deluge.

XIII

SPRING CLEANING

A LENT like this is almost the earliest possible. Those who prefer the moods of nature to sympathise with the moods of the Liturgy will regret it. We Christians are soul plus body, saved by an Incarnation; and it is an over-scrupulous spirituality that labels our submerged instinct of nature-worship wholly pagan. If Lent corresponds more or less with our English spring, begins with the spring sowing and ends just when mid-April gives shy hints of the coming foison of the year, so much the more comforting; so much the easier to enter into the spirit of Lent as a sacrament of our renewal.

Not that you can leave out the idea of penance; Lent is ploughing time as well as seed-time, and cannot dispense with the rude March blasts of pulpit exhortation. But it is also a season of renewal, a recurrent supernatural spring. The message of Easter cannot flood the mind with hope as it ought to, unless there has been preparation made for it, laborious and uncomfortable.

It is our human instinct, in springtime, to make some special effort by way of getting back to where we were. The ancients, according to their own medical theory, let blood, or at least took a purge, to be rid of their accumulated poisons. We (in peacetime at least) subject our houses to the rigorous discipline of broom and duster; a yearly penance for the studious mind. Not otherwise, we prepare for Easter by a long and painful dusting of our consciences, which is Lent.

27

STIMULI

Our Lord must cleanse the Temple twice, once at the beginning of his ministry and once at the end of it, so prone were his go-getting contemporaries to encroach, undeterred, on the sanctities of the Temple. So we human temples need to be purged not once in a lifetime but at regular intervals; the dust of our misplaced affections is always accumulating unobserved.

This year—let us hope, not again in our life-times—the fast of Lent is abrogated. In a world which already imposes on most of us so much of austerity the cruder forms of self-denial are perhaps out of place. Not out of place are those private resolutions for keeping Lent by which, as by a kind of nursery self-torment, the ingenious piety of the faithful loves to take discipline.

Those small reversals of our daily habits which, viewed as mortifications, would seem so petty, have their value if they jolt us, ever so little, out of the comfortable rut our lives have grown into. Some lessening there must be of minor distractions and dissipations, if our consciences are to have their spring-cleaning.

XIV

THE SOWING

ANYBODY would have told you, if you had asked in Jerusalem on the first Palm Sunday, that Jesus of Nazareth was at the height of his popularity. It even looked as if his reputation was destined to go beyond the limits of Palestine. Some Greeks, who had come up to Jerusalem for the feast, expressed a desire to see him. If we may use a modern comparison without irreverence, he was in the position of some popular leader nowadays when the foreign journalists begin to take notice of him. What was the " interview " he gave them ? A curious one. " The hour is come for the Son of Man to be glorified. A grain of wheat must fall into the ground and die, or else it remains nothing more than a grain of wheat ; but if it dies, then it yields rich fruit."

Our Lord Jesus Christ did not come to earth to share our crowns. The pageantry with which he rode into Jerusalem was not what it looked like, a bid for popular leadership. Rather, it was a kind of satire on worldly success ; he would heighten the contrast between that whirl of popularity in which he lived, and the lonely contempt in which he died, by a dramatic gesture. Those palms should lie trodden in the dust for days afterwards, to remind the world how brief are its triumphs. He had come to earth to die. His human body should be lodged in the earth like a grain of wheat, to yield the splendid harvest of his Resurrection. And it was our Resurrection, as well as his ; we were to see with our eyes, handle with our hands, the mystery which still

29

baffles our understanding, the law of death in life and life in death.

It would not be difficult to illustrate that moral by an allusion to those many countries in the modern world which lie dead, awaiting their Resurrection. But perhaps the best way of keeping a day of intercession is to look beyond the immediate prospect which drives us to our knees. Holy week should be a week of holydays—holidays from the problems and fears which occupy our thoughts. Your soul is a grain of wheat which must fall into the ground and die, on pain of sterility ; only by a death to self and a Resurrection into the world of grace can it become fruitful for God. We must enter into the joys of Easter by entering into the sufferings and the death of Christ. Entering into them, not by way of artistic appreciation, not by merely feeling sorry about it. We were buried with Christ in our baptism ; we are dead, and our life is hidden with Christ in God. Our business this week is to associate ourselves with Christ's Passion, to unite ourselves with the dispositions of will and purpose with which he emptied himself, annihilated himself, in our name. Self has to be dragged out and crucified.

XV

ON SECOND THOUGHTS

NOTORIOUSLY, the Resurrection narrative in
Luke and John is complicated for us by one odd
circumstance—it insists that the risen Christ was
not easily recognisable on first view. This
allegation has been exploited before now by authors who
wanted to make out that the Resurrection appearances
were illusory. The point was ill taken; if it is true that
recognition of their Master reached those first witnesses
gradually, not immediately, to that extent the evidence for
the fact in dispute becomes stronger.

There is nothing disconcerting, to be sure, about the
statement that the apostles in the upper room " thought they
saw a spirit." They may have recognised the features of the
Intruder, but fallen back, understandably enough, on the
hypothesis that it was a *revenant*. Yet we may notice, for
what it is worth, that this is the reverse of a ghost story.
Almost always, the narrator of such a story thought at *first*
he was seeing a real person; only later did the impossibility
strike him. Here it is the other way round; the claim that
it was a real Person depends, not on a random impression
but on a considered judgment.

The earlier appearance to the Magdalen is even more
significant. It is a familiar experience to be thinking hard
about X, to be interrupted suddenly by Y, and, at least for
a split second, to mistake Y for X; it is as if the train of
thought could not run down without a slight time-lag.
Once more the process is reversed on Easter morning;
the Magdalen is so far from identifying the source of the

interruption that she projects the idea of a gardener-sexton to account for it. Voice and features alike only sort themselves out upon reflection.

With the disciples on the Emmaus road, the time-lag is much more remarkable. There is a longish conversation : besides, what more reveals the tricks of a known personality than sharing a country walk ? Only at the last moment do you get the instinctive recognition followed by the reflection that, if they had only thought, they would have known it all along.

There was more excuse for the apostles at the lake-side. The Stranger hailed them as " Lads! " (not as " Children!"); he was some way off ; and there may have been a mist. But the same consideration applies ; it was not the distant Figure on the shore, it was their Host at the *al fresco* meal that reminded them of a lost Friend.

Natural explanations have been suggested, less attractive than St. Gregory's view—that the witnesses suffered from a miraculous inhibition, proportionate to, and significant of, their inadequate faith. But no explanation makes the evidence less singular or less impressive.

XVI

HIDDEN WITH CHRIST

"YOU HAVE undergone death, and your life is hidden away now with Christ in God." Baptism, in St. Paul's thought, is a drowning, followed by restoration to life of the apparently drowned.

The man who went down into the waters of baptism might be conceived as taking his last look at the heathen world he was abandoning. What a hideous world! All the cruel circumstances of slavery, and most men were slaves; lust cultivated everywhere and by every artifice; the unscrupulous hunt for riches; dumb gods obscenely worshipped. There was just a moment of oblivion, when immersion in the chilly water cut him off from all his surroundings, and then he came up out of the water, a new man, living in a new world. They were there still, the familiar objects of sense, the wharves, and the noisy market-place, and the temple pediment crowning the hill. But all that meant nothing to him, was nothing to him, now. The piece of nature that went down into the water had undergone death, and a newly created thing had taken the place of it. His life, now, was hidden away with Christ in God.

I like to think of the Christian soul as a fugitive; let us say, a runaway slave, with the pursuers on his track. He is standing before the door of an open grave; yonder, opposite him, is a shelf clearly meant as the resting-place of a corpse, but no corpse is there. Something, however, there is: a long winding-sheet, and a veil so wrapped together, you can see it once went round a man's head.

He draws the winding-sheet about him, throws the veil over his head, lies down on the narrow shelf, waiting, listening. There is a tramp of horses outside. " No harm taking just a look in here, anyhow." Then a dark shadow blots out the sun-light, and he must hold his breath till he hears, "It's all right, there's nothing in here, only a dead body."

When the dark shadow of temptation falls across our view, I wonder if we use that resource as much as we might? I mean, lying close and reminding ourselves that we are dead to all that kind of thing. Somebody has injured you, and you feel inclined to let yourself go in a passion of resentment : perhaps you can see a way in which you might get " even " with them. You feel you can't let the injury pass : you owe a kind of duty to yourself, to see that the other person doesn't get away with it. Then is the moment to remind yourself, " I am dead, and my life is hidden away with Christ in God."

XVII

A LITTLE WHILE

ALL St. John's Gospel is baffling; none of it
more so than the extracts which are read out,
these Easter Sundays, from the altar. " What is
this *little while* he speaks of ? " the apostles
asked ; and, despite the explanation given, their bewilderment is echoed by generations of commentators. Only, as
usual, there are strands of comfort floating, as it were,
under the surface ; you are still not quite clear what the
apostles were meant to think about it all, but what *you* are
meant to think of it does, albeit elusively, emerge.

Dream-fashion, you connect it with the alternations of
light and shade that a normal April brings with it ; those
comings and goings of our Lord after his Resurrection,
have they not the very quality of spring ? " Rabboni ! "—
" My Lord and my God ! "—" Lord, thou knowest I love
thee! "—one moment of ecstatic recognition, and he is
gone.

Alternations occur, not less poignant, in the history of
souls that have enjoyed close intimacy with God. Now it
would be Eastertide with them, and they would come
running back to tell us of high experiences, too high, alas,
for our dull understanding. Then the sun would be withdrawn, and they would be left in the drab twilight of
Ascension-tide, gazing up, hungrily and hopelessly, at the
cloud that hid him from their sight. Commonly, to be
sure, that would not be the order of it ; with most of them
it was privation first, fruition afterwards. But not always ;
for St. Theresa of Lisieux, all through her last days, the

shadows were unrelieved. For Père Clugny, Ascension Day was the best of all feasts ; you congratulated the absent Christ with wholly disinterested love.

Some of us, on a much lower level, are apt to chart, over-anxiously, the alternations of cloud and sunshine in our lives ; the times when prayer comes easy, the times when we merely set our teeth and hang on. But what basis have we for computing, in this connection, our expectations of the anticyclone ? *Horas non numero nisi serenas ;* best imitate yonder sun-dial, that counts only the bright intervals.

XVIII

DIVIDED TONGUES

A PIOUS Jew from Cyrenaica, on pilgrimage to Jerusalem for the Feast of Weeks, was passing up the Street of the Chain about nine o'clock in the morning, when he observed several little groups of men shouting aloud as if under the influence of some uncontrollable emotion, to the astonishment or amusement of the bystanders. As he approached the first group, he found that these men, peasants from the country, were talking neither the Aramaic he knew, nor the Greek he used on his travels, nor the Latin which was his familiar tongue. The second group were still more of a surprise ; one of them, quite distinctly, was talking in the Berber *patois* he learned as a child from his nurse! That is, unimaginatively put, the story of Pentecost.

" How is it that we hear them speak in our own tongues?" —the miracle was discussed, naturally enough, in terms of its miracle value. But the question which suggests itself as we look back on the story is a *Why?* It is hard to believe that there were any pilgrims in Jerusalem at the time who knew nothing but the language (say) of Cappadocia ; hard to believe, therefore, that the glossolaly had any merely practical purpose. Rather, it was a Divine gesture. And it is easy to see that the beginning of a Universal Church was a suitable moment for repealing the curse of Babel, for making men forget their differences of nationality. But the curious thing is that the miracle, if anything, emphasised nationality. Peter got up and addressed the onlookers, presumably in Greek of the *koine*, and they all

37

seem to have understood. Indeed, the known world of that period was nearer to having a common culture and a common speech than it has ever been before or since. What the miracle did was, apparently, to drag to light these half-forgotten local dialects which Greek, at the time, had almost superseded; to make men Cappadocia-conscious, when for years they had been thinking of themselves as cosmopolites. That, surely, needs explaining, if we can be hardy enough to demand explanations when Heaven is at pains to lavish its portents.

Is it fanciful to suggest that a Church launched under such auspices must have been conscious of a mission to be at once international and national? To override distinctions, without obliterating them? This is, after all, the characteristic genius of Christendom. Mahommedanism appears in history as a culture that subdues, Christianity as a culture that absorbs. Neither Jew nor Greek, neither barbarian nor Scythian—and yet the Church has stood by the cradle of all the European nations and sponsored them; sponsors them still. A hazardous, but a Divine commission.

XIX

THE UPPER ROOM

FOR ONE set of people in history, one particular room must have had vivid and crowded associations. Those people were the apostles and the first Christians, a hundred and twenty in all, who were gathered in the Upper Room on the day of Pentecost. They could remember how they first came into it. Six weeks back, their spirits already overcast with tragedy. Almost immediately, their Master warned them that one of their own number would betray him. There is nothing more unsettling to man's whole being than the sudden discovery of treachery in his fellow man. And worse still was the terrible whisper of doubt in each heart, " Lord, is it I ? " And then the washing of the feet, and the Sacramental Meal.

In that room they reassembled, an hour later, panic-stricken fugitives. They, who boasted that they could drink the chalice of the last ordeal, meet there, in hiding. The only sorry boast of their party is Simon Peter . . . and then the door opens, and he, too, joins them, his face furrowed with tears. The apostasy is complete.

In the same room they met again, three nights afterwards. Through the twilight of their doubt came flashes of hope. The Tomb has been found empty ; there are stories of a re-appearance. There will be trouble over this with the rulers ; best keep the doors locked. And suddenly, through those locked doors, he whom they had abandoned returns, gives them his peace and his pardon.

A room haunted with memories ; through that door,

39

Judas crept out into the night; on that table the consecrated chalice reposed ; through that window they listened to the shouts of " Crucify him !" ; that stone on the floor has been trodden by impassible feet. It was in these surroundings that the Holy Ghost came. The inspiration he brought was to be something altogether new in the world's history, yet it was to be based upon, and rooted in, memories of the past : " When he, the Spirit of truth is come, he will bring all things to your remembrance." The scene of their inspiration for the future was to be a scene enriched by past experience.

Inspiration and experience, how seldom they go hand in hand! *Si jeunesse savait, si vieillesse pouvait* . . . . So it is with the religions of the world. There are Eastern religions with an immemorial antiquity, which have no instinct to urge them forward, no vital power of self-adaptation. There are new religions in the West, which begin their careers full of an intoxicating initiative, but they have no roots in experience, and they do not last. With the Church it is otherwise. In those six weeks before Pentecost the Apostles had already lived through, as it were, the whole cycle of Church history; there was nothing callow, nothing tentative, about their earliest *démarches*. And because she was born old, the Church remains ever young. She retains the memory of the Cenacle and the Catacombs, yet for her Pentecost is continually repeating itself, making all things new.

XX

THE CHRISTIAN CHURCH

THE Christian Church is the detonation of that explosive for which a train had been prepared through the centuries. Everything that happened before the day of Pentecost was a kind of dress-rehearsal for the day of Pentecost. That influence which the Holy Spirit had hitherto exercised sporadically, picking out here and there a mouthpiece suited to his ends, he now began to exercise within a delimited sphere, under agreed conditions, with calculable results.

In our human experience, a spirit does not function normally without a body to which it is attached, its coefficient, its counterpart. And until the Christian Church came into existence, the Holy Spirit (like Wisdom in the Proverbs) had no home among men; there was no Body to be his means of self-expression. " The wind blows where it will "—that was the *whole* truth, when our Lord spoke; the activities of the Holy Spirit were altogether unconfined, altogether incalculable. Now, he has a Body through which his activities are normally mediated.

Baptism, the Sacraments, the life of grace—it has all been brought within our human compass. This or that exterior action we perform, and the invisible assistance of the Holy Spirit infallibly accompanies those actions. It is a very impoverished Christian life which tries to attain union with God in entire isolation. We are meant—all our documents proclaim it—to find ourselves as members of a Spirit-filled, Spirit-actuated Body ; if we remain in its unity, we know that the life of the Spirit is, however imperceptibly, expressing itself in us.

All this is not to suggest (absurdly) that Pentecost limited, canalised the operations of the Holy Spirit. It remains true that he blows where he will ; we know nothing of the way he comes or goes. When we said he spoke by the prophets, we did not mean that in the rest of creation he was dumb. And if he animates the Church, that does not exhaust his infinitude.

XXI

THE BLESSED TRINITY

WE ARE too apt to let the prayer value of the Christian mysteries pass us by. How can they aid us in prayer, these remote doctrines which defy the familiar currents of our thought? At the best, they will distract us ; at the worst, we shall be led away into heretical speculation. Yes, but mysteries are not barren impossibilities. They are truths hazily perceived, like the tantalizing half-memories you retain of last night's dream. And they can float, at least, on the surface of one's prayer. It is not a bad prelude to any devotional exercise, to put yourself in the posture of praying in union with the Life of the Blessed Trinity.

You can begin by reaching out towards God the Father, as the unutterable Source of all being ; try to get outside of yourself, replace that busy, agitated self which is the centre of all our thought by the naked idea of God. He is the ultimate Centre and Term from which existence flows and into which it flows again. You can want to be nothing and to feel as nothing, in comparison with and in the presence of that ever-awing Personality.

And then—it will be clearest for our present purpose if we reverse the proper order, not of precedence but of procedence—you can think of the Holy Spirit, under the figure of all that stir and motion which God sets up in his creation as a response to himself. You can make of him, as it were, not the object but the subject of your thought ; be conscious of his part in your prayer by envisaging him,

43

not as the God to whom we pray, but rather as the God who prays in us.

And in the third place, with more difficulty perhaps, but with the consciousness that it is St. Paul's own doctrine, you can think of the Divine Word as the self-expression, everywhere, of the eternal Father, and therefore, here and now, his self-expression in you. In him and through him, our Head and Representative, you reach upward towards the Centre of all being. You have come into God's presence to offer yourself to him, and, once you are there, find after all it is not yourself you want to offer, a thing so miserably insufficient. Rather, in your place you want to offer God his own Son, tabernacled in your heart and putting his infinite worth at your disposal—Jacob in Esau's disguise winning the Father's blessing, but for Esau. God above you, God at your side, God within you—a mirror of that Divine Life by which the three Persons of the Godhead eternally subsist.

XXII

THE SACRAMENT OF PEACE

JERUSALEM, the psalm tells us, is built like a city which is one in fellowship. Palestine lies across one of the great strategic highways of the world. But Jerusalem itself stands remote among the hills, as if to let the rumours of world-history pass it by. Meanwhile, its inhabitants, so cut off from commerce with their kind, were to be bound together by strong ties of civic unity; it was to be the city of peace. A grand destiny, imperfectly fulfilled.

Like the Jewish temple, the Christian altar is the rallying-point of God's people. The whole notion of Christian solidarity grows out of, and is centred in, the common participation of a common Table. The primitive Church in Jerusalem broke bread day by day from house to house; its stronghold of peace was not any local centre, but a common meal. Christian people, however separated by long distances of land or sea, still meet together in full force, by a mystical reunion, whenever and wherever the Bread is broken and the Cup blessed.

War is a sword; it brings division into our lives. It has sundered the nations; it can interrupt the exchange of commerce, of ideas, of diplomatic courtesies. It cannot interrupt the current of sacramental fellowship which unites us with our fellow-Christians when we and they share the same heavenly banquet. Years may have to elapse before the external conditions of free intercourse are re-established between us and our friends abroad. But as children round our Father's Table, we are already at one. Our friends yesterday, our friends to-morrow—in the timeless existence to which the Christian altar introduces us, they are our friends to-day.

War has divided families and circles of familiar acquaintance. So many children living separated from their parents : such difficulty in meeting our old friends—a sense of isolation is creeping over us ; we cling to anything that will unite us to one another. Must we not cling, above all, to the Sacrament which provides us with a real opportunity of making ourselves one with those we love ? In absence from our homes, in perilous places, in prison, it may be, or in exile, we are still united, all of us, unless the barrier of unrepented sin or dead faith intervenes.

Bitterest of all, at such times, death comes close to us and breaks up our familiar human groupings. But it has always been the instinct of the Church that death itself cannot dissever the bond of sacramental unity. There is remembrance, at the altar, of God's servants and handmaids who now sleep in the sleep of peace, leaving us to watch in the wakefulness of war. An empty place at table, and an empty chair by the fireside, but not an empty place at the Communion-rails; that Sacrament which unites the living unites, somehow, the living with the dead. Neither life nor death can separate from the love of Christ us or them.

XXIII

THE RELIGION OF THE HEART

JUNE IS the peak month of the flower-year; and visitors to our churches register disappointment when they find our best floral effects distributed round the Sacred Heart statue. Of all our statues, commonly, it has the least artistic merit; pose, features, and colouring indicate that the repository has gauged, all too accurately, the popular taste. The visitor, if he does not share our creed, is apt to exclaim, " How unevangelical! How un-English !"

He is wrong on both counts. " The Heart of Christ in Heaven towards sinners on earth, or, a Treatise demonstrating the gracious Disposition and tender Affection of Christ in his humane Nature now in Glory, unto all his Members under all Sorts of Infirmities, either of Sin or Misery," was written by Thomas Goodwin, a Cambridge man, victim of the Laudian repression and chaplain to Oliver Cromwell.

There is nothing unevangelical about the devotion to the Sacred Heart. No, the question raised by Thomas Goodwin is, How far can Christian devotion legitimately go in the direction of the sentimental ?

It is a kind of approach that scandalised at once the Jansenism of Port Royal and the robust Anglicanism of the Warburton school; and it was really a matter of good taste. Theologically, you cannot drive a wedge between the human and the Divine Nature in our Lord for the purposes of worship. But it is possible to concentrate on the Sacred Humanity with an intensity of imaginative affection which some critics will inevitably label sentimentalism.

STIMULI

" As sweetly as doves do converse with doves, sympathising and mourning each over other, so may we with Christ, for he thus sympathiseth with us " ; that is Goodwin's claim, but there will always be a kind of up-stage Christianity which finds fault with such demonstrations. Who are we (it will be asked) that we should dare to feel *sorry* for the Crucified ? And such minds will suspect that the bad art (for it is, mostly, bad art) springs naturally from a wrong fount of devotion.

Is there, quite apart from theological orthodoxy and unorthodoxy, a right and a wrong approach in such matters ? Can we suppose there is good taste and bad taste in devotion, as in the arts ? And if so, ought the views of those who have good taste to be a canon, as in the arts, for those who lack it ? I am unashamedly glad to be able to leave such questions unanswered.

XXIV

THE TRANSFIGURATION

TUCKED away in a fold of the year when people are most apt to be on holiday, the feast of the Transfiguration is on the whole little regarded. The story itself stands out very much as an interlude in the Gospel history : a moment of lightning, thunder and cloud, and we are back in realities again ! Yet the first three gospels conspire to make it prominent ; and all agree on the moment of it, six days (St. Luke says about a week) after St. Peter's confession.

It has been suggested that the whole scene took place at night ; that is why the apostles woke from sleep in the first instance to see what they saw. But this detail would hardly have gone unmentioned. No, in broad daylight, while our Lord was at prayer, the glory that dwelt in him suddenly shone through. Two men, afterwards identified as Moses and Elias, stood there talking to him about his Passion. Peter urges they should make a feast of Tabernacles of it, building three arbours there. A cloud descends, a voice comes from it, and when the cloud has passed, all is as it was before.

The theological moral is sufficiently indicated in II Peter, 1 ; the appearance of Moses and Elias, with the voice that appealed to their witness, confirmed the apostles more than ever in their conviction that our Lord was the fulfilment of the Old Testament prophecies.

Meanwhile, the scene suggests another consideration. There is a well-known picture (Raphael's, I think) which represents on one canvas the Transfiguration above, and the possessed boy in agony below. All our three accounts tell us that this was the sight which met our Lord's eyes immediately on his descent from the mountain, and the contrast which the picture deliberately offers is at once legitimate and salutary. All is peace above, all chaos underneath. The feast, after all, is not inappropriate to holiday-time; our Lord is for once taking a holiday from the multitude. Peter suggests the prolongation of this holy holiday; " Lord, it is pleasant being here. "

His suggestion is not rebuked, it is ignored. And the silence which greets it is the answer, surely, to the question which perpetually raises itself in our minds, whether it would not be a better thing for Christians, individually or in the mass, to remain perched on their mountain-top of prayer, and let the world go its own way; can it do any good, interfering? There are times at which the figure of the possessed boy makes a good type of the world we live in. But we know that all but a favoured few of us have to come down from the mountain; holidays come to an end.

XXV

THE EMPEROR TAKES HIS COAT OFF

HOLY Cross Day, which recalls the defeat of Chosroes and the return of the true Cross to Jerusalem, has one specially gracious detail about its legend. It must have seemed eminently appropriate that the emperor Heraclius should dress up in his best robes and carry the sacred relic back into the city; and when he found himself unable to move, at the very threshold of the gate, the troops must have looked very straight in front of them while the vulgar craned their necks; nothing so embarrassing as an elaborately staged ceremony when there is a hitch in it. Bishop Zachary's guess proved the right one, that the robes must come off before Heraclius was worthy to carry the emblem of a crucified Master; and, with no more dignity than Hans Andersen's emperor, he finished the journey in his shirt-sleeves.

History was repeating itself; about seventeen centuries earlier, King David had brought the Ark, type of the Cross, into Jerusalem, and in such scant attire as made the scornful Michal, at her window, accuse him of dancing like a mountebank. His instinct told him, without any priest to jog his elbow, that royalty did well to unfrock itself in the presence of the Infinite. Born into an age when debunking is the fashion, let us not forget that it cost something to demean yourself exteriorly, in days when the world cared more for these pomps. Even St. Francis, when his father disinherited him, and he dressed up in an old sack, mortified himself, I think, as well as the old cloth-merchant.

We moderns are contemptuous of outward appearance;

it does not follow that we are humble. Clothes, after all, are only (as it were) a sacramental manifestation of the instinct we all have, to hide our defects from the world's scrutiny. The "folly of the Cross," the placarding of our human weakness, is something more intimate than the mere stripping off of outward paraphernalia.

It means being ready to let the world see you as the fool whom God sees, whenever a suitable occasion arises. And it is humiliating to think how much of our unpublished thought process is devoted to doing just the opposite— trying to put ourselves in the right, to mask our ignorances, to explain away our failures, to pretend that the *gaffe* meant something else. Oh, we laugh at ourselves in private, that costs us nothing. We even amuse our friends, and cultivate a reputation for modesty, by dwelling on the record of our own discomfitures—afterwards, when we are in safe company. But really to put aside our self-esteem, and follow, stripped, in the footsteps of a stripped Master— that is a rarer gift.

XXVI

NOT AGAINST FLESH AND BLOOD

WE ARE all tempted to leave the invisible world out of sight. Granted that there are supernatural beings, angels and devils, native to an immaterial order of existence, are we any the better for letting our minds dwell on the fact? Surely we have enough to do fighting evil, bolstering up good, on this earthly battleground of sense which is our own theatre of hostilities? Enough for us to do our bit in the particular sector of the line entrusted to us, not concerning ourselves with the strategy that is being worked out, far beyond our ken, by the Higher Command?

It is easy to talk such language. But now and again—Michaelmas Day gives us, above all, the opportunity—we do well to take a larger view, and see our little world of dust and striving in its true proportions. If only for this reason, that it helps us to see Good and Evil in their pure form as two forces eternally in conflict, one fighting to preserve, one to destroy, the whole of God's creation. It helps us to detach our notion of them from those human prejudices which are apt to distort the view.

Contemplate the figure of a warrior Saint, driving his spear into the dragon that lies coiled at his feet. "St. George," you tell yourself; and it is not long before you start putting an ideological or a controversial name to the dragon. We do not easily forget our prepossessions; we are more than a little akin to Mark Twain's savage, who, when the missionary told him that Cain was a South Sea

Islander, asked, " What was Abel doing, fooling around there, anyway ? "

It is certainly bad for our peace of mind, possibly bad for the world's peace, if we are content to decorate all our experience with these party labels. St. Augustine reminds us that when we give vent to our indignation against a fellow mortal, we are commonly treating our own brother as an enemy, without knowing it ; only the devils are so black that we can despair of their salvation. So, in Chesterton's *Man who was Thursday,* the detectives continue to mistake one another for anarchists. It is well to remind ourselves, on Michaelmas Day and perhaps at more frequent intervals, that our warfare is not against flesh and blood, but against principalities and powers that belong to a different order. The moral issues we are fighting out here are only the image, refracted by our finite views, of the real Life-and-Death conflict. Put wings on that figure of the soldier-saint, and he is transformed from St. George into St. Michael ; enough to make us pause, and wonder whether we were being a little parochial.

XXVII

MICHAELMAS

DEVOTION to the Holy Angels has its ups and downs, like the other devotions of Christendom. In the first age of the Church the tendency was to exaggerate it, and some of the earliest heretics were condemned for paying to created spirits an honour which is due only to God. In the Middle Ages Michaelmas was one of the principal events of the year, marked by festivities hardly less important than those of Christmas itself. Nowadays it is little remembered except as a quarter day, not always a day of rejoicing. Not, surely, because it is difficult to believe in the existence of angels ; it would be a very ill-balanced creation if there were no immaterial spirits to match the brute creation, matter without spirit. If anything it is Man, the half angel, the half beast, that taxes our credulity by existing. The difficulty is not to believe in angels, but to remember about them.

Yet a devotion to these inhabitants of a different world is calculated to encourage three important attitudes of mind—detachment, humility and confidence.

The appearance of angels to mortal eyes, a thing constantly asserted both by scripture and by tradition, is not so much the intrusion of a new factor upon the scene as the revelation of a fact already present.

> *The angels keep their ancient places ;*
> *Turn but a stone, and start a wing!*
> *'Tis ye, 'tis your estranged faces*
> *That miss the many-splendoured thing.*

C   55

STIMULI

We are so impressed with the multitudinous richness of this visible world that we forget the existence of anything else. If it ceased to bully the imagination, our thoughts would find it easier to fly upwards.

And again, we are so self-centred, so self-important— like an old lady who has lost a parcel in the post and forgets there is a war on. If we could only see creation as a whole, we should realise that there are spiritual intelligences in which God has reposed depth upon depth of wisdom ; that there are angelic creatures whose whole nature is penetrated with transports of burning love. " O God, in whose presence the angels stand, hear thou " (incidentally, as it were) " the prayers of thy servants."

And again, the ministry of the angels inspires confidence. We are wrong if we think of that ministry as a merely New Testament affair ; surely, if it was needed then, it is needed much more now ? " Not of Gennesaret, but Thames "—there is no incongruity, only unfamiliarity, about the notion of Jacob's ladder pitched between Heaven and Charing Cross. God knows it is hard, in an inhumanly mechanised age, to see the events of our lives as planned. But have we, theologically, any alternative ?

XXVIII

CHRIST THE KING

I T IS with some effort of the imagination, nowadays, that we picture to ourselves what is meant by the royalty of Christ. He is, *ex hypothesi,* a king whose right does not take its origin in any way from the consent of his subjects. He is what he is only because he is the Son of his Father. Here, at least, is royalty inherent in the person. There are many countries, there are many hearts in which Jesus Christ does not rule. But everywhere he reigns ; over every human heart he claims a king's title to obedience. As he stood before Pilate in the praetorium, the man who lolled there in front of him was his subject.

Asked whether he is a king, he says, Yes, I am. But he does not stop there : " What I was born for, what I came into the world for, is to bear witness of the truth. Whoever belongs to the truth, listens to my voice." Belongs, not merely by right of origin, not merely in the sense of partisanship. The man who belongs to the truth takes his character from it, reproduces it, his whole outlook is dominated by it. His answer to the question " What is truth ? " is a simple one—truth is everything. If Pilate had belonged to the truth, he would not have been content to spend a few hours on a spring morning playing with his conscience. But truth was not in his line ; he was only a politician.

It is the nature of truth everywhere that it enjoys sovereignty over the human mind. You can run away from it, shut your eyes to it, but it reigns in spite of you, has a royal claim to recognition, which does not depend on your acceptance of it. Truth as it exists in God's mind has a royalty of its own ; banish it from the earth if you will, by police measures, but it will still reign, a monarch in exile.

Pilate was truth-shy ; a practical man in search of a formula, he turned tail and ran from the judgment-seat, to escape the challenge of those calm eyes. There is a temptation for the men of our own day to imitate his attitude ; so much to be done, here and now, in this visible, tangible world. Their fathers, half a century ago, were for ever worrying about religion, desperately concerned to know whether there was truth in any creed, and if so how much. Today we have despaired of the quest, and turned to other things. But Jesus Christ still stands among us, a prince incognito, waiting to be judged, and we postpone the trial—cannot he see how busy we are ?

XXIX

ALL SAINTS' DAY

THE MEANING of the word " saint " has narrowed, but used to mean everyone who was in heaven or was going there. It is now only used of those whose lives were such that the Church can tell us for certain they are in heaven. (She never tells us for certain that anybody is in hell.) They died as witnesses to the Christian faith, or they showed in life such love of God, such contempt for the world, that they were living advertisements of the creed they professed. God set his seal on them by doing miracles on their behalf ; he wanted them, not merely to be good people, but to be known to be good people. Their light was not hidden ; their neighbours came to learn the truth about them, honoured them, and asked them for their prayers.

" Saints," then, is a term which does not cover all the inhabitants of heaven ; it neglects the presence, there, of uncanonised millions. Whom do we celebrate on November 1—the canonised saints ? Or all the people who have crept in somehow as we hope to ? St. Thomas of Canterbury, St. Richard of Chichester, and St. Henry of Bavaria ; or just Tom, Dick, and Harry ? I have little doubt that the Church is thinking of the former. Yet (as long as we do not pretend to know their names) there is nothing to prevent us honouring all the rogues who have made a good end. For myself, I like to think, on November 1, of an intermediate class.

By an odd custom, the Pope sometimes elects Cardinals *in petto*—that is, he never divulges their names ; the historian Lingard is said to have been one of these. I like to think that God sometimes elects saints *in petto* ; that there are souls of saintly, or almost saintly, calibre, whom he wants (for some reason) to go unrecognised among their fellow-men. Especially I like to remember a few whose path has crossed mine in this dusty world, whose contact suggested, to my very fallible judgment, the suspicion of sanctity. I do not mean simply people who are very unselfish, very patient under misfortune, and so on. Thank God, there is a great deal of unexplained goodness going about, and we have all met plenty of people who make us ashamed of ourselves. But there are just a few people who have that touch of the supernatural about them which corresponds to genius in literature, to "charm" in common life ; a breath of the other world seems to hang about them. For these obscure luminaries let us thank God once a year, not less than for the bright examples which come to us reflected by hearsay.

XXX

THE RESTLESS

IS IT an experience all of us have, or only some of us, to be unable to enjoy your seat in the chimney-corner because somebody else is roaming about the room, moving things, looking for something? I suppose there are a variety of reasons for it; but one, surely, is the consciousness, or the illusion as the case may be, that you ought to be roaming to and fro yourself, doing something about it.

The modern world is chiefly spoilt, for us comfortable ones, by the same sense of communicated restlessness. You may be disposed, by age or temperament, to let the modern world go its own way, curl yourself up and make what nest you can out of the sticks and straws of a civilisation. But the effort is vain; what defeats you is the sense that the world is in disequilibrium.

I had thought of heading these lines " Displaced Persons." But, while the tragedy of homelessness is real and persistent, that is not all the tragedy; there are so many Misplaced Persons. It is a common fate to be out of harmony with the whole order you live in, to be astrain with unrealisable political ambitions, to accept the pattern of things around you, but not to acquiesce in it. A restless world, infecting the most sedentary of us with a twinge of unrest.

Perhaps the twinge is good for us. We are not meant to be wholly at ease, and it is part of our completion to be exercised, a great deal of the time, over the fate of other people. That is why one month in the year is set aside for an uncomfortable occupation; for remembering that easily forgotten class of humanity, our dead. Here and there death cannot be imagined, for a moment, as anything else than a shining transition. Usually it is otherwise; our instinct, on hearing that our friends have been displaced from this world of visible experience, is to picture them as misplaced persons in whatever lies beyond. They fitted in so suspiciously well with this pattern of mortality; can the imagination easily devise a future world in which they will find themselves at home?

A Christian tradition which goes back, demonstrably, to the Catacombs is our warrant for believing in an intermediate state. We comfort ourselves with the belief that the dead still live, only to make ourselves uncomfortable by the reflection that many of them cannot, as yet, be in a state of equilibrium; we have to pray that they may find rest. Not least when Armistice Day comes round to remind us, felicitously enough, of those many who died as victims, to secure for us whatever of civilisation is still left.

XXXI

THE BONFIRE

SOME of our Lord's parables seem more difficult to understand the more you read them. Not because their meaning is elusive, but because a forest of alternative applications grows up round them, and you find yourself asking, in honest bewilderment, which is the primary, the obvious application. So, not least, with the parable of the tares (or cockle, or darnel, or whatever it was) among the wheat.

Straightforwardly enough, it answers the problem of evil—so far as that problem is intelligible to minds which cannot create, and therefore do not understand the conditions of creating. This world is a world of probation, and to such a world scandals (in the Scriptural sense of the word) are as necessary as obstacles are to an obstacle race. The tidying-up process which our sense of justice demands is something that must be looked forward to in the future. But then, why this mention of the kingdom of heaven; that is (regularly in the parables), the Church? A fresh vista opens itself; you begin to read the answer to the equally familar question, why Christianity doesn't work better. If Christendom is the nucleus, the raw material of heaven, why does not heaven shine out more luminously in the lives of Christians? The answer, plain enough, is that any organised Church gives you not gold waiting to be minted but ore waiting to be smelted; there will always be dross.

Yet none of us would willingly put down one of our Lord's parables content with a mere theological lesson;

there must be at least a gleaning from it that is meant for our own individual lives. Here, too, the tares are recognisable enough, discernible from the wheat but not easily separable! How closely intertwined are the roots of good and bad motive, or at least of good and of indifferent motive, in our conduct! How tainted our very asceticisms are with pride, our very altruisms with love of interference! All that is clear; but what is the policy of the Good Husbandman? Does he always leave both to grow together till the harvest? Not always; there are lives in which we see his mysterious weed-killer of pain so effectively used that death (to our view at least) seems to bring with it a hundred per cent. wheat crop. What happens when that does not happen?

That the soul, when death comes, has its eternal destiny settled, we cannot doubt. But must the wheat be swept into the garner, tares and all? Is there no separating process still needed? And if there is, will it be painless there, so painful here? And if not, should we not remember, in this month of bonfires, the faithful but imperfect dead?

II

A FEW SAINTS

I

THE DIVINE WISDOM

IN THE book of Proverbs, the Wisdom of God is represented as telling, in her own person, the story of the world's cradletime. You see her represented as an architect, surveying a heap of ruins where destruction has left nothing but a heap of masonry, carrying the plan, ready shaped, of the wide streets, the magnificent houses, that are to rise there when the rubble has been cleared away.

While the mountains rise in their majestic outline, while the sea shrinks to its appointed limits, while the springs burst out to water the parched hill-side, she, God's Wisdom, is there, plays over the scene like sunlight over a pool. And her delight was to be with the sons of *men*. Man, the crown of all God's works, was to be the spectator and the beneficiary of the rest.

The liturgy recalls that scene of God making the world, then illustrates the scene of God remaking the world. It is a very different one ; you have to imagine a peasant woman, a little way to the west of Nazareth, looking out over the plain towards Mount Carmel, outlined against the sunset. A little Boy stands beside her, just learning to talk ; she teaches him to say " mountain."

Or, to the east of Nazareth, she and he come to a gap in the hills, where he catches his first sight of the Lake of Galilee, a thousand feet below ; he learns the word " sea." Or she goes out with him to draw water from the spring, the only spring at Nazareth ; it is still called the Fountain of the Virgin, after her ; one more word for his vocabulary.

STIMULI

And his day-dreams are of the city he will set on a hill, the net he will cast into the sea, the fountain of living water that will spring up from the believer's heart.

Is it a kind of self-importance which makes us feel in these times, every Advent, as if a new Advent were needed to straighten things out for us, take our world to pieces and put it together again? We know, really, that we are only given one second chance, that the redemption which came to us from Nazareth has potentialities in it which will rebuild the world of this century, as surely as it rebuilt the world after the Dark Ages. We shall get no help from looking up to other hills than Carmel, catch nothing in other seas than the Lake of Galilee, find no other answer to our thirst than the fountain at Nazareth.

God knows we need his Wisdom, if we are to make anything of our rubble-heap. But she is near us; her delight is to be with the sons of men.

II

" BY HOOK OR BY CROOK "

IN LUKE V, after bringing his apostles miraculous success in their fishing, our Lord says to St. Peter, " From henceforth thou shalt catch men." In John xxi, upon a similar occasion, he says to St. Peter, " Feed my sheep." What account are we to give of this curious irrelevancy?

Our Lord, risen from the dead, is reclining with his apostles by the lake side, sharing a meal with them. I do not know of any picture in the gospels which breathes more of security and content. It is likely enough that somewhere, on the hill, a shepherd was to be seen looking after his sheep. Peter looks up at him and pities him—such a dull life, the shepherd's ; the lambs and their mothers to be fed by hand, the shearlings to be led out to pasture, year after year. How much better to be a fisherman, to face the angry elements, to manage your boat, to have a catch, once in a way, like to-day's catch !

Our Lord sees the same picture, with different feelings. He remembers how Moses, just before his death, asked to have a successor appointed to carry on his work. " May the Lord God of the spirits of all flesh provide a man that may be over this multitude, and may go in and out before them, and may lead them out and bring them in, lest the people of the Lord be as sheep without a shepherd." Our Lord is in the same position ; can he, the Good Shepherd, leave his flock to stray as it will, without some visible representative to rally them, some accent of an authoritative voice ? " Feed my lambs . . . Guide my shearlings . . .

Feed my sheep." You, Peter the fisherman, are henceforward to be Peter the shepherd ; all that anxious, plodding care which the shepherd gives to his sheep, you are to give to the faithful, looking after them, when you would much rather be spreading your net to catch men's souls.

Peter, to be sure, was a fisherman ; he was to go out and conquer souls for his Master. But he was marked out from the first as the organiser, the pivotal man who was to keep the infant Church together, to set up, first at Antioch and then at Rome, a *See*, a sitting-down-place from which he could superintend the work of others. He envied sometimes, I suspect, the free-lance activity of St. Paul ; initiative is a more alluring vocation than responsibility. There will have been dull days for the fisherman turned shepherd. And it was an irony of Providence that Peter, of all men, should have been chosen for this governing, this moderating part. The impetuous schoolboy hero of the gospels, who blunders so attractively, takes risks so explosively, to turn into the safe man, who must smooth over difficulties, settle disputes, offend his subordinates by over-caution!

The world has to be saved by hook or by crook ; it is well for the Church when anglers and shepherds do not fall out.

III

THE CONVERSION OF ST. PAUL

I SUPPOSE there is no case on record in which the coming of first grace to a human heart is so violently manifested as in that of St. Paul. It came to him against his will. None of us likes to look a fool, and who was ever in such a humiliating position as the young Jewish theologian when he came to Damascus, a blind man asking for a Christian missionary to baptise him ? It came to him quite unforeseen. It is possible that he was in bad faith, kicking against the goad ; we are so mysteriously fashioned, we men, that sometimes we do persevere in what we know is wrong, telling ourselves all the time at the tops of our voices that we know it to be right. But he had not calculated on the possibility that Christian faith might come to him when it came. And the result was a complete change of his whole life and his whole scale of values. His first reaction, when he realises he is beaten, is, " Lord, what wilt thou have me to do ? " He asks at once for orders from his new Employer ; grace does not simply check him in his mad career ; it hurls him violently, all at once, in the opposite direction.

First grace comes to us undeserved ; that is evident. Are we to suppose, then, that it cannot fail of its effect ; that, since he has called us, God will see to it that we come safely to him ? No (says St. Paul to the Corinthians) ; being baptised is like being entered for a race in the hope of winning a prize—but there are the also-rans. I myself, he adds, run all out in this Christian race of mine, fight my round cautiously; I mortify my body and bring it into subjection,

71

for fear I myself should be counted out. (He was named after King Saul, the first and disqualified king of Israel.) To make the start is one thing, perseverance another.

He reverts to the metaphor of the racecourse when he is writing to the Philippians. I don't look behind me, he says, like an unskilful runner ; I keep my eyes on the long stretch before me, the long distance I have to cover, if I am to reach the goal of perfection God means me to reach. " Perseverance " doesn't mean merely a kind of jog-trot which will get us there in the end if we stick to it. It is a progress, a growth ; giving yourself up more and more to God, fitting your life more and more into his pattern.

And at the very end of his life he returns to the same metaphor again. " I have fought a good fight, I have finished my race, I have kept the faith " (a friend of mine thinks it means " saved my deposit "). He is to receive the victor's laurel-wreath from a Judge who awards it justly. No one ever regretted less a fall from the saddle.

IV

CALLED AWAY

A TOLL-GATHERER sat doing business at some petty *octroi* in Galilee. His name was Levi, and we should still think of him as Levi if he had not written a gospel himself and given away his Christian identity. Renamed Matthew at his conversion, he would mortify the sense of shame by calling himself so from the first. Yes, Mark and Luke were right; it was Levi who sat at the receipt of custom. But it was not Levi our Lord saw sitting there; he saw (as Matthew tells us) Matthew. He sees in us not what we are, but what we are to become; and we become that because he sees it in us.

Zacchaeus, a rich man and the chief of the toll-gatherers, publicly offered restitution of his ill-gotten goods when he gave himself to Christ. Matthew simply rose and followed, leaving the money to lie there. Perhaps he was only a subordinate, learning his nasty trade. Anyhow, he had no thought but for his new apprenticeship.

The Emperor Julian criticised the apostles for the illogical promptness with which they rose and followed a Stranger, knowing nothing about him. Did they know nothing about his miracles? These things were not done in a corner. If they knew nothing, at least we know nothing about the majesty of that presence, the smile of welcome in those eyes. Some of the least repented decisions of our lives were taken, not after laborious weighing of pros and cons, but under the influence of some personality which made us say instinctively, " I am safe here."

With St. Matthew, there were other grounds for con-

73

fidence as well. Why had the Stranger's choice—if it was a Stranger—fallen on him? He was nobody's hero, a despised Jew to the foreigners who passed, a despised publican to his fellow-Jews. To see a job that wants doing is often the first intimation you have that this is your job ; to recognise somebody else's need for friendship can, in the same way, be the first intimation that you have found a friend. " If *he* can find any use for me, there must be some fatality about it, some pre-concerted harmony of wills ; nobody else has ever wanted me." That is the argument at its lowest.

But there may have been another reason. He could tell that the road which led him to follow Christ was the right one, because it was the road which led away from the customs-house. It was otherwise with the fishermen ; St. Matthew was perhaps already sick of petty extortion ; it was his chance to escape. Sometimes, not always, God shows us the right way only by showing us that the opposite way is, for us, wrong. The silver, glinting in the sunlight, shone on the beckoning Figure ; the memory of ill deeds illumined, by contrast, that other life to which the road lay open.

V

A FRIENDLY FIGURE

I HAVE never had the chance to panegyrise to-day's Saint, St. Barnabas. His feast is nearly always in occultation through the incidence of one movable feast or another. Let me give a vignette of him here, by way of compensation.

Men of a heroic age, the New Testament saints have sometimes a daunting effect on us, their weaker brethren; we are afraid they would be difficult to live up to, make us feel uncomfortable, if we actually met them. St. Barnabas is of the heroic stature; alone, outside the circle of the twelve, he and St. Paul are honoured by the liturgy as "apostles"; and one pictures him as in actual presence a more commanding figure than St. Paul, or why, at Lystra, did they identify him as "Jupiter"? Yet every mention of him seems to bear out the first notion you are given of him, in Acts iv, as a "man of encouragement." It dates, no doubt, from the very practical encouragement which he, a rich man and a Levite, gave to the despised Galilean movement. But you feel sure of that encouraging quality when St. Paul comes back to Jerusalem after his conversion, and is given the cold shoulder by the authorities of the Church. Doubtless they had every reason to fear him as the persecutor of yesterday, perhaps the *agent provocateur* of to-day. St. Barnabas "took him" (the verb probably implies the overcoming of a certain diffidence) and forced his company on the older apostles, the ideal protector of a shy convert.

He is the ideal *entrepreneur*, too; he has an eye for

75

greatness in others, and goes off to look for St. Paul as soon as there is an opening for the gospel among the Gentiles at Antioch. He is content to be eclipsed ; when they preach in his own country of Cyprus they are " Barnabas and Saul," but on the mainland they are " Paul and Barnabas." When they quarrel (a comforting reminder to us that holy men can quarrel), St. Barnabas is typically on the side of leniency—they must not drop his nephew St. Mark simply because he did not stay the course on their first journey. Later on, St. Paul thought better of the strict line he had taken ; it was St. Barnabas who by instinct, from the first, would consider persons rather than principles.

In times of crisis, under the stress of moral preoccupations, we are all apt to label people black and white, refusing to listen to any plea in favour of the former category. But it is questionable whether the apostles of a new world would not do well, in our day, to find room for a Barnabas or two among their number.

VI

CAREFUL AND TROUBLED

IN THE story of Mary Magdalen there is something of dramatic and literary value which is not content to appeal to a merely Christian public. Her feast fell on July 22; a week later, with very little enthusiasm even on the part of Christians, we commemorate that practical, bustling sister of hers, St. Martha. It takes all sorts to make a heaven.

Mary sits at her Lord's feet; meanwhile, with her clear head and capable hands, Martha flounces in, a little contemptuously; the type of all good presbytery housekeepers, the type of all good women who have ever tried to make a prophet comfortable in spite of himself. She resents male incompetence; why cannot the disciples look after their Master better? She resents Mary's demand for spiritual refreshment; cannot she see how tired their Guest is?

That calculation, surely, lay behind the request that Mary should help with the serving, plate-breaker as she probably was. Our Lord sees through the plot; smiles (you can see him) as he sums up the difference in psychology between the two sisters. " Martha, Martha, how many cares and troubles thou hast! " You are right, but you have not seen all. Blinded by your own self-sacrificing impulse to do what you can for me, you (like the woman of Samaria) have forgotten to ask what I can do for you. The ideally best is to be got out of life in Mary's way, not (so far as it is distinguishable) in yours. You must learn to lean before you can learn to help.

STIMULI

So much our Lord says in defence of the Magdalen; it is she that is being attacked. And the Church, all through the centuries, has been careful to defend the contemplatives against their critics. If you are privileged to enjoy, here, a foretaste of heaven, that is for you the unrefusable call. That has to be emphasised, because the world is always more prone to sympathise with Martha's attitude. But the Church's rebuke, like our Lord's, is not for those who bustle, but for those who grumble; not for the business-like, but for the busybodies. Martha's work too is very dear to our Lord's Heart; she is the patroness of all those holy people, in the cloister and out of it, whose charitable bustling makes the world's ends meet.

There is fussiness, there are petty jealousies; human beings are human. But when all is said and done, Martha's is a noble and a necessary work, and we should be nowhere without her. It is only that she must learn not to criticise; she will do her work better if she keeps her eyes on the tray. Then, in the least of his brethren, let her welcome Christ.

VII

THE UNDERGROUND MOVEMENT

OF ALL the martyrs, only St. Laurence is commemorated by that gospel which is so eminently appropriate to martyrdom—our Lord's words about the grain of wheat falling into the ground. Perhaps because he represents the Church of the Catacombs, when our religion did quite literally have to go underground. Anyhow we read it, somewhat out of season, in August.

"A grain of wheat must fall into the ground and die, or else it remains nothing more than a grain of wheat; but if it dies, then it yields rich fruit." A good test of whether a man knows his Bible is whether he knows the occasion of this utterance. It was on the first Palm Sunday; the procession was just over, and some Greeks asked to see the Hero of the day. A decisive moment, when the fame of a local patriot has spread far enough to justify foreign journalists in asking for an interview. The statement issued to them must have been something of a puzzle.

Obviously it is central to all our faith as Christians. You are not a Christian in the most rudimentary sense unless you believe that the Death which happened on Good Friday was somehow the liberation of Life on a world scale. There is a curious thrill of revelation when you dig up the first tentacled white lump which tells you that the winter wheat has begun sprouting. The heathen had experienced it, and guessed dimly at the possibility of a resurrection. Our Lord never despised the guesses of the heathen; he simply wrote R against them.

STIMULI

Central to the faith of the martyrs, and of those puzzled contemporaries who watch the martyrs go to their deaths, with more misgiving than the martyrs themselves. That their blood is the seed of the Church—it has been repeated so often; can a thing which has been repeated so often as that really be true ?

Central to that individual faith in which the Christian lives his own life. He only begins to stop being mystified by the ways of God to men if and when he realises that the most mortifying (good word!) setbacks which he experiences on the surface of his religious life are evidence that God is at work on his sanctification deep underground. Not only when he prays for blessings which are not, apparently, granted. Deeper than that; his moments of something akin to despair, when it seems as if the Christian promises could not be meant for him ; moments when doubt catches at the fringes of his mind, questioning whether there are any Christian promises, for him or anybody else— what is all that but grace working underground? But it is slow work.

VIII

SAINT PATRICK

THE SAINT whose festival so many people of English speech are celebrating was, beyond question, an ascetic. "We are told," says the official obituary of him, cautious for once, "that he recited the whole psalter every day, and every day worshipped God three hundred times on bended knees. He divided the night into three portions; during the first he went through a hundred of the psalms, the second he spent immersed in cold water, finishing the other fifty, and in the third took his meagre rest, lying on bare stone."

How much of this programme (there is more of it) the saint really observed, how often and for how long, is not to my purpose. Enough that this is the picture of him his disciples have built up; presumably this kind of asceticism is in his tradition. It was like him to die in Lent. Irish spirituality must not be assessed by what we can remember of "Father O'Flynn"; there is a hard streak in it, and there are few pilgrimages in Christendom where the old rigours are practised as they are at Lough Derg.

For the fiftieth time you catch yourself wondering, Were they made of tougher fibre than ourselves, physically, those giants of old? Or did they lay too much emphasis on external activities, mistake means for ends? Or does Chesterton's "St. Francis" do well to remind us that the men of the Dark Ages were doing penance for the sins of paganism? Or does the complicated setting of our modern lives dispense us from imitating the heroic? Or are we, by and large, a poor lot?

STIMULI

Probably there is something in some of our excuses, though commando warfare made one suspect that the first has been overdone. We have pin-pricks to endure of which a pachydermatous generation was unconscious; the temptations against which we crave to be fortified are more of the spirit, less of the flesh, than theirs. And certain it is that asceticism is meant to make the will function properly; to abstain, under doctor's orders, from going to church is for some of us a mortified proceeding. The pity of it is that the remorseless energy of the saints (at least as painted with the firm brush of their biographers) is apt to prove a discouragement. *Le meilleur est l'ennemi du bien*; can we really think of ourselves as "imitating" St. Patrick if we abrogate in Lent those five or ten minutes of wondering whether to get up or not?

At the risk of anti-climax, let me deprecate this feeling of discouragement. A life which leaves no room for physical self-denial in its programme lacks, it is to be feared, either humility or love.

IX

THE MERCIFUL KNIGHT

YESTERDAY'S saint, St. John Gualbert, is canonised in the popular mind by an incident of his unregenerate days as The Merciful Knight. Meeting his brother's murderer on Good Friday, he granted him life in memory of our Lord's Passion: and when he turned aside to pray before a crucifix, the Figure of the Crucified bowed its head in greeting. Burne-Jones depicted the story. Shorthouse borrowed it for " John Inglesant," and it is remembered accordingly.

Butler's " Lives," incorrigibly orthodox, give you to understand that the knight set out to do something very wicked, and was induced to repent of his design. But it may be questioned whether, by the standards of his age and society, he had not a right, and even a pious duty, to punish the murderer when the opportunity offered. The Merciful Knight we call him, not The Law-abiding Knight, and it takes the edge off his performance if we picture him as belonging to a police-ridden age like our own.

If he showed mercy, as opposed to mere self-restraint, it must surely be supposed that in his own conscience he would have felt justified in striking the blow. A right was his, and he forwent it. Nowadays, criminal procedure has become mechanised, to the great advantage of the community, and if somebody murders your brother or mine, no representations on our part can save him from the rope. But it was the age of rough justice that produced the good stories.

In modern law, mercy in the strict sense finds no place. True, the jury may recommend a criminal " to mercy," but what they are really thinking of is equity, a notion as old as Aristotle. There were extenuating circumstances, the prisoner had a good war record, *therefore* the death penalty should be remitted. But there is no " therefore " about mercy in the strict sense; it forgives where no motive can be assigned for clemency; equity corrects justice, mercy overrides it.

Or rather, in St. John Gualbert's case, there was a motive but it had nothing whatever to do with the criminal. He forgave because it was Good Friday, and the name of the Crucified had been appealed to. The mercy he showed was thus an authentic echo of the Mercy we all hope for at the last, won by the merits of a Divine Redeemer, not by our own. You and I can show mercy, of a sort, by renouncing a hundred mean little expedients for " getting our own back." We cannot forgive on the grand scale; only God can do that, for he is at once Judge and Plaintiff.

X

FIRE

S T. IGNATIUS, who died on the last day of July, nearly 400 years ago, was described by John Wesley as " surely one of the greatest men that ever was engaged in the support of so bad a cause." John Wesley was exactly wrong. He thought to defend the founder of the Jesuits from the charge of " enthusiasm " by representing him as a cool, long-headed business man. But an enthusiast was just what St. Ignatius was. He was full of that fire which never says " It is enough."

Read his early history, and you find nothing there of the great organiser. All his great schemes for going out and converting the Sultan (copied from St. Francis) came to nothing. All his early disciples left him: " thou couldst a people raise, but couldst not rule " seemed to be his destined epitaph. In a sense, it was the enormous vagueness of his plans that saved the situation ; just because he had no blueprint ready formed in his mind of what the Company of Jesus was to be like, the Company of Jesus proved to be exactly what was wanted.

If, during the last years of his life, he became the ruler of a world-wide Society, that was because he was a good enough Jesuit to accept the uncongenial task. The real charter which he left to his Society was not any set of rules. It was a set of meditations, chiefly on the following of Christ, which he composed when he was living as a hermit in the cave of Manresa. All that mattered was seeing the love of God as insatiable.

We live in times when great importance is attached to planning, and Christian people are apt to catch the infection from their surroundings. We must revise, we must re-organise, we must have a plan, or we are lost! But I don't think St. Ignatius would encourage us to echo that cry. Rather, he would find fault with our half-heartedness—ready to believe, to do, to spend just so much and no more. But the fire never has enough.

III

THIS AND THAT

I

PHARISEE AND PUBLICAN

TWO MEN went up into the temple to pray;
two men, each, in God's sight, just an immortal
soul, although their circumstances, their training,
were so different. One a Pharisee, highly respected,
scrupulous, fastidious, a man of rank; and the other a
publican, nobody's friend, nobody's hero, all his thoughts
wrapped up in his business, and that business certainly a
sordid, perhaps a dishonest one. Both went up into the
temple to pray; religion has that great gift of levelling
us; it takes all sorts to make a Church. Went up, separated
themselves from the busy din of the streets, isolated themselves for our inspection. We can watch them easily;
deep in their devotions, they will not suspect that they are
being watched.

And the Pharisee prayed thus *within himself*—he was too
well-bred to pray out loud; but our Lord has told us the
thoughts that passed through his mind. " O God, I give
thee thanks "—come, that is a good beginning; he acknow-
ledges his dependence, he recognises that he is highly
privileged. " That I am not as the rest of men "—quite
true; he has had a good education, a high family tradition;
he has much to be thankful for. " Extortioners, unjust,
adulterers "—was it really necessary to underline his own
negative virtues ? " Or even as this publican "—yes, that
gives the whole thing away. He looked so absorbed in his
prayers, didn't he ? But that was only part of the performance : all the time he was looking out of the corner of
his eye at the shabby figure over yonder, and despising him.

" I fast twice in the week, I give tithes of all I possess "
—what is the use of saying all that ? He went up to the
temple to pray, but he forgot his errand ; he was too busy
in contemplating his own good qualities to find time for
petition. Two men went up to the temple, but only one
prayed.

And the publican ? He stood far off, so as not to disturb
the quality at their devotions. He did not dare to lift up
his eyes to heaven ; he was too full of shame to challenge
scrutiny. He smote upon his breast, for all to see what
manner of prayer was his. He may have been a kind father
and a good friend, but it does not occur to him to mention
all that. He sees himself in God's sight only as God sees
him ; God be merciful, though man be unmerciful, to me a
sinner.

We can put a name to the Pharisee: he was called Simon,
and he comes in the seventh chapter of St. Luke. We can
put a name to the publican; he was called Zacchaeus, and he
comes in the nineteenth chapter of St. Luke. Zacchaeus in his
tree, the Magdalen kneeling on the floor, the publican
beating his breast in the temple court, all give us the same
clue ; the door of heaven is low, and we must stoop to
enter it.

II

DISINTERESTED LOVE

FATHER D'ARCY'S new book, *The Mind and Heart of Love*, threads for us anew an old maze of controversy. Is the motive of love, in the last analysis, to give something or to get something? Is not love profaned by the suggestion that we yield to its influence because we want to derive some advantage from it, however noble, however spiritual an advantage, for ourselves? On the other hand, can the sacrifice of self be in the true sense a motive? Is love desirable only because it is the highest fulfilment of ourselves? Or must we learn to disregard the question whether love is desirable or not?

Father D'Arcy tackles his subject at a high level of philosophy; we may be pardoned for attempting to answer the same problems in the light of common sense and of rudimentary piety. Left to himself, the lover is insistent that nothing of self enters into his calculations; it is for herself alone that he loves the lady of his choice. If he never saw her, never heard from her again, his life should still be immolated to the cherished memory of her. What he desires is her greater happiness and perfection, not his own. But, confronted with her, dare he talk the same language? Has he the courage to insist that the long hours he spends in her company are intended to provide satisfaction for her, not for himself? Such altruistic advances would, it is evident, be coldly received. He will be better advised to represent himself as a humble pensioner on her bounty.

As with human love, so with divine; there is an apparent contradiction in it which cannot be escaped; we must look

it in the face. The Quietists, and Fénelon in his champion-
ship of the Quietists, would have it that the love of God
should be wholly disinterested, " the love that asks not
anything, love, like thy own love, free." They were prepared to sacrifice their own salvation, if that were demanded
of them, to prove themselves true lovers. On the other
side, much Christian piety (especially of the Evangelical
type) takes man's need of salvation as its point of departure ;
cannot imagine approaching God except in the attitude of
a suppliant asking favours for itself. Which is the more
truly Christian approach—the generosity which refuses
to ask for anything, or the humility which refuses to do
anything but ask ?

Perhaps, after all, in human love the conscious motive
is altruistic, the unconscious motive our own well-being.
But in Divine love ? I think we shall be well advised to tell
God that our love of him is self-regarding, and we wish
it were not.

III

SIGNIFICANCE AND INSIGNIFICANCE

YOU, WHO read this, are the target of observation from a hundred different angles. You are like a celebrity landing in a foreign country, surrounded by camera-men.

To the statistician, the mass-observer, you are one unit in a crowd. To the physicist, you are a mathematical formula, to the chemist a compound of substances, to the biologist a specimen. The behaviourist sees you as an animal modified by conditioned reflexes ; the psychologist as a mental type suffering, to a more or less degree, from morbid variations ; the philosopher, as the subject of a conscious experience. You interest the historian as one of the innumerable insects that build up the coral island of human development ; the economist, as bee or drone that helps to cross-fertilise the cycle of production and consumption. To the postman, you are an address ; to the tradesman, a ration-card ; to the politician, a voter ; to the revenue, a tax-payer.

You are surrounded by specialists, each of whom invites you to take a look at yourself down his own particular microscope. Choose which you will, the prospect is discouraging. In any given relation, from any given point of view, what relevance you have is only the relevance of a cypher. You feel like a small boy just arrived at his first school, and given to understand by the matron that he is Locker Number Ninety. Each science catches man from one particular angle and makes a fool of him, like the snapshot which gives you your portrait arrested in mid-walk.

STIMULI

Allow any one of the specialists to buttonhole you, consent to look at the world down his pet vista of observation, and your own shadow, to be sure, will look attenuated enough. But there is another side to the picture. Ask yourself for a moment why it is that all these observers are concentrating their various spotlights on *you*, and it will give food for more comforting reflections. Whether or no Man is heir to all the ages, he is certainly the common target of all the -ologies. Man alone has a finger in every pie, challenges the attention, at long last, even of the astronomer. How significant a being we must pronounce him, after all, this focus in whom so many rays meet ! And do not say that *you* are only one among the others; you, no less than any other, are integral to the sum of humanity, indispensable to the species. The fact is, each separate spotlight only catches one facet of your external relations ; the inner core of you is something beyond their cognisance.

So significant you are, so universally relevant. But how, and by what right ? Beware of asking ; that way lies theology.

IV

THE WAITERS

WHY DOES the Authorised Version, in to-day's epistle, give us, " He that ministereth, *let him wait upon* his ministering "—the italicised words being supplied so as to give the sentence grammar ? " Let him confine himself to " is rather the thought ; St. Paul is obviously hitting at people who mind everyone's business except their own.

Did the compilers, in an inspired moment, take their cue from to-day's gospel ; from the servants at Cana of Galilee who were told to go on and on drawing water, and see what happened ? " Ministers " the old Douay called them ; for indeed the word is the same in the Greek ; Bishop Challoner, revising the Douay, altered it to " waiters ". Curiously, when he got to the Romans, he did not tell us to " wait " upon our ministering—he might have said " wait upon our waitering."

If St. John gets mystically interpreted, he has only himself to thank for it. And it is impossible to think of those waiters at the wedding-feast toiling with their buckets to fill six water-pots and then (Westcott is surely right) going back to the well for more, without being reminded of the day-to-day, hand-over-hand pieties of the ordinary Christian, content with what the world thinks drudgery if he may cherish the hope that, some day, grace will intervene, turning the water into wine.

I am not thinking so much of the clergy. Heaven knows, plenty of our time is spent in waiting for results which don't seem to come. But our neighbours accuse us of our

unventuresomeness, and I must not provoke controversy by
extolling the rut. No, the ordinary Christian much more,
trying to bring up a recalcitrant family on decent lines, to
influence, vaguely, an unresponsive circle of friends, to get
the better of his or her own bad habits, feels the drudgery
of the often-repeated task. Not least so, with Pie-crust
Sunday coming to remind us of already broken resolutions.

Why do we admit to ourselves so little the feeling of
staleness which is half the difficulty of the Christian battle ?
Spared from so many recent dangers only to be like the
Gibeonites, hewers of wood and drawers of water in God's
service ; the monotonous clank of the pump-handle deafen-
ing and deadening all that was once gracious and spon-
taneous in our approach to religion ! All this makes it
useful to be reminded, as year after year begins, of that
dogged second-best which is required of us as a minimum.
That grace, in this life, will ever transmute the water of dull
effort into the wine of inspiration is more than we dare to
hope. Elsewhere, perhaps, we shall understand the baffling
simplicity of the command, " Fill the water-pots with
water."

V

CATTINESS

ST. PAUL'S great outburst in recommendation of charity is one of those epoch-making pieces of literature which have altered language. Our language, at any rate ; the word " charity " has derived from that circumstance a specialised meaning. Not the crude meaning, which suggests the great lady of a period not ours going round distributing coals and blankets to the poor ; you can distribute all your goods to feed the poor, and yet have no charity. No, that other specialised meaning in which " charity " approaches nearly to " tolerance," although it throws mere tolerance into the shade by being something more positive, more dynamic. You show charity, in our favourite English sense, if you really try to make allowances for the man who disagrees with you, really try to enter into his point of view.

St. Paul was not, I think, using the word in any specialised sense. He mentions, in this particular context, certain dispositions to which, incidentally, the love of God gives rise ; and because he is writing to the Corinthian church, torn with factions and lost in admiration of rival prophets who will not even queue up and take their turn, he draws attention to what we, with our loose English habit of speech, call " sins against charity."

At the same time, perhaps because he was a man continually involved in controversy against his will, I think St. Paul is apt to concentrate attention on this special quality the love of God has—it makes for fellowship. Sometimes you are even tempted to translate *agape* " fellowship " in his writings ; so definitely they foreshadow that later Christian *argot* which would talk of a man as presiding over the *agape* in the city of the Romans, the Communion in a double sense of Christian people.

Anyhow, it does us no harm to have these familiar words read out to us on the threshold of Lent, that thumbnail sketch, so admirably dashed off in a few breathless clauses of the Christian person we would like to be and aren't. At the moment, when subjects of disagreement are many and feelings are beginning to rise high, we have to be on our guard against the kind of factious spirit which makes us see everything in terms of our propaganda against the other fellow's. It is not an impossible Lenten resolution to give up, for a matter of forty days, the delights of saying " I told you so " ; to cut out from our conversation, where it has almost a firmer hold than in our minds, the spirit which I think St. Paul, if he had talked modern English, would probably have labelled " cattiness."

VI

ISAAC AND ISHMAEL

REFRESHMENT Sunday's epistle bothers us for several reasons. St. Paul is juggling with two allegories and a single application; roughly you can say his formula is— as Sinai is to the Mount of the Beatitudes, so the earthly Jerusalem is to heaven, so the Law is to the Gospel. Again, we do not, like St. Paul, see Christianity against a background of recalcitrant Judaism. Finally, the notion of some men being born to freedom and others to slavery is no longer, for us, a practicable metaphor.

But most of us have, from an early age, contrasted the characters of Isaac and Ishmael without (it is to be feared) experiencing the proper reactions. That concise description (fourteen letters in the Hebrew) " his hand against every man, and every man's hand against him " offered an attractive vignette of a man (or nation if you will) holding his own by rugged independence. Isaac, by contrast, was the most sedentary of the patriarchs; you could not be enthusiastic about him. Yet somehow, at Mid-Lent, we were expected to congratulate ourselves on being like Isaac and unlike Ishmael. The sort of people we admired at school were so plainly, we felt, of the type St. Paul mentions with disapprobation. . . .

In any case, Ishmael was surely *freer* than Isaac? So we reasoned, but of course we were getting St. Paul all wrong. To-day's epistle contrasts, not two types of character, but two destinies, the earth-born and the regenerate. The application is not moral but allegorical; the Law (St. Paul claims) was only a kind of caretaker

99

Government, an interim arrangement until the gospel should come ; just as Ishmael was a kind of interim arrangement with which Abraham was forced to make do until Isaac was born. Ishmael may or may not be the noble savage ; the point is that he is only an untidy second-best, he is not the real thing.

Our schoolboy prejudice about the two types was partly right, partly wrong. Right, because the niggling, un-adventurous Christian has reason to be dissatisfied with himself. Wrong, because the splendid egoist is only a literary admiration of ours ; in real life, he is *de trop*. But all that is beside our present mark. Philosophically, no doubt, self-pleasing is slavery, self-control is freedom. But all that is on the natural level ; St. Paul is pointing us to a different kind of freedom, that supernatural birthright of ours which opens wider windows altogether for us, the heirs of eternity. No need to state the thing in terms of crowns and harps ; the Christian rests, here and now, on a confidence in the reality of the Unseen which liberates the springs of his soul. It is in that spirit that the Church gives us Laetare Sunday in the middle of Lent.

VII

CHARITY

THE EPISTLE for Quinquagesima Sunday is perhaps the best known passage in St. Paul's writings, but not necessarily the best understood. The Corinthians are very proud of their spiritual accomplishments—speaking in strange tongues, known or unknown. Less satisfactory news is that these highly mystical people are continually quarrelling among themselves (no, it is not impossible). St. Paul tells them that unless they have charity their spiritual manifestations are no more use than a jazz band. What, then, is charity? Giving away money (he is going to appeal for the collection in the next chapter but two)? No, you can give away everything, without having charity. Going to the stake for your convictions? No, pride will easily persuade you to go to the wrong stake. Charity does the sort of things pride or ostentation will never do; is humble, gentle towards others, forgiving, understanding, and so on; loves the truth, and hangs on in spite of despairs. Now at last we think we have got it; charity is just " comfort in another's troubles, courage in your own "? No, that is not all St. Paul means; the rest of the epistle shows that. He begins to contrast it with the other two " theological " virtues, showing that he means love of God, manifested in love to your neighbour, not love of your neighbour simply. Charity is the luggage we shall take to heaven when we have left everything else behind ; and there will be no troubles in heaven for us to meet with courage, or lighten by comfort. Charity is love of God, the thing we were built for.

STIMULI

The most profound mystical experience possible on earth is, compared with the experience of heaven, what baby-language and baby-thoughts are compared with the mental processes of a full-grown man. Faith and hope belong, evidently, to a world in which the whole machinery of the spiritual order is something we have to take on trust. Even knowledge—and that, for St. Paul, does not mean book-learning; it means all that any Saint has ever had of God-consciousness—must disappear in heaven, like a candle's light when the blinds are drawn up. We shall *know* in heaven, but altogether differently; not by the same medium as here. But love is not discontinuous; it bridges time and eternity.

Have we got it, this love of God which ranks higher than anything else we can have? Best not consult our feelings; they are an indifferent guide in such matters. If we are curious on the subject, it is better to turn up I Corinthians xiii, and read verses four to seven again. Do they strike you as a blue-print of the way in which your life is actually lived? It is not a complete test, but it is the best available.

VIII

OUR TOYS

THERE are certain situations which impel us, at the risk of platitude, to moralise. One of these is Removing; the moment when the door of the pantechnicon slams on the last of your ill-assorted worldly goods, and it takes the road—an ark freighted with that little world of tangible memories which is to bridge the gulf between yesterday and to-morrow.

An added pathos forms an undercurrent to the sadness of your good-byes; the pathos of having surrounded yourself and, worse than that, linked yourself, with all this retinue of material belongings, a few of them cherished, the rest retained only because wise friends assure you that " you can't buy them nowadays." How abominable (you think at one moment) to be so carelessly rich in a world full of homeless human beings, euphemistically labelled " displaced persons "! How you envy, at the next moment, the holy religious who flit from one house of their order to the next with no more luggage than a suitcase! And behind it all, a certain premonition of mortality; " he shall take nothing with him when he dieth "—the pantechnicon is too much of the same family with a hearse to make you feel quite comfortable.

Is our instinct of possessiveness a failing, an imperfection of which we should do well to accuse ourselves? At least it is something very deeply rooted; witness the tight grasp of the infant's hand on the toy from which bed-time must part it. Sometimes you wonder whether there is not something in the suitcase, a book of piety perhaps, which even the holy religious relinquishes with a pang when year by year, according to a gracious custom, he makes a gesture of restoring all the trumpery things he possesses to their communal ownership.

Let us not belittle the sacrifice he makes, by telling ourselves that the desire to have things is in itself wrong. Few minds are so pedantically wedded to a political theory as to believe it. To be sure, they are only toys, the things we grown-up people are loath to part with. But the very fact that they are toys is our excuse for hugging them.

Rather, it may be surmised, we should aspire to detachment ; a cultivated readiness to do without anything God sees we should be better without. Only we must not reckon (like the remover) in terms of avoirdupois ; detachment is concerned, not least, with the imponderables. The claim we have staked out on So-and-so's affections— *that* is more worth renouncing than the photograph-album, the pincushion which might come in useful. Detachment is of the heart.

IX

REVELATION

"ONCE you were all darkness; now, in the Lord, you are all daylight." It is common to talk of revelation, in the old-fashioned sense, as if it had merely added to our previous knowledge of divine things; a series of " dogmas ", hard to believe and impossible to prove. But its effect was, no less importantly, to assure us about the truth of what we believed, or half-believed, already. " All darkness "—Man troubled with a soul, haunted by race-memories of Paradise; and yet incapable, when it came to the point, of sticking to a sane theology, or of living a consistent morality. Now lapsing into silly idolatries, now working himself up into a condition of passionate hate of the very mention of the word " God ". Now enslaving himself to a set of meaningless taboos, now throwing into some unworthy, some blood-thirsty cause the heroism which should have been devoted to the service of mankind. Is there room, in a rationally governed universe, for the existence of a creature so blinded by the rush-light of his own half-knowledge?

If you would gauge the difference which revelation has made to our notions of worship, you have only to concentrate on a single *obiter dictum* of Aristotle's. " We should think it very odd," he says, " to hear anybody talking about loving Zeus." He is discussing friendship; love is not properly so-called where there is no hope of being loved in return; you do not, therefore, " love " in the true sense an inanimate object, such as your dinner; nor, for the same reason, a Divine Being.

STIMULI

The exchange of love between God and the individual human soul is to be found, sure enough, in the Old Testament. A dozen times in Deuteronomy, eight times in Ecclesiasticus, thirteen times in the rest of the Old Testament writings. The prophets tell you to fear God, to seek God, to come back to God, not to love him. Mankind is still under tutelage. It was not till the full revelation came to us that we were spoilt with this sense of a Divine intimacy. I use the word " spoilt " advisedly : for indeed this sense of intimacy is now something we take for granted. Even your half-Christianities, which dislike the idea of revelation and will not tie themselves down with historical assertions, insist loudly that the love of God is the only thing which matters. They are kicking away the ladder they climbed on. It would not have occurred to them to love God, if something had not happened in the first century A.D. The really staggering demand which revelation makes on our powers of belief is when it assures us that God wants to be loved.

X

THE STIRRUP AND THE GROUND

THE EPISTLE and gospel of Septuagesima, unlike those of most Sundays, form an obvious pair. In the epistle, St. Paul warns the Corinthians not to imagine that they are indefectibly established in grace; they may yet fall away. It is never too late to lose grace. In the gospel, the labourers who find their way into the vineyard, and are treated with the same generosity as those who have borne the burden of the day and its heat, clearly indicate the possibility of a last-moment reconciliation. It is never too late to find grace. Time casts dreadful shadows on eternity; a consideration to make one pause, even if Septuagesima does not happen to be also one's birthday.

The moral, to our ancestors—to the men, say, of John Wesley's time—seemed plausible enough. People played for high stakes, and an evening's entertainment could easily send a rich man to the debtor's prison. On the other hand, the death-penalty was common for minor offences, and the petty criminal might always hope for a reprieve. The idea of losing everything, winning everything in a moment was easily entertained. "As the tree falls, so shall it lie" was a favourite quotation; naturally it was your dispositions at the hour of death that made all the difference.

In our day, Pelagius has supplanted Calvin. If we ourselves were giving a testimonial (say) to a boy leaving school, we should not expect him to be judged by the frame of mind in which he took his departure. We should average out his conduct over a period of years. May we not expect

Divine Justice to do the same; give us marks (to put it crudely) on a lifetime's performance, and sum up accordingly rather than concentrate on a death-bed attitude? The more so, when we reflect how many old people, for better or worse, do not live up to their previous reputations. People are apt to be scandalised by the story of the Penitent Thief. And what of the complementary picture—the sudden death of an unaccustomed sinner?

But the gospel, if we let it speak for itself, has hard edges. We do not know that God ever condemned a soul for an isolated sin, but we should be fools to doubt that he might. We do not know if the lines, " Betwixt the stirrup and the ground, Mercy I sought, mercy I found," describe a frequent occurrence; but many of us would be sorry to doubt that they do. If you entertain doubts about the morality of death-bed repentances, ask yourself what you would say to a dying man expressing sorrow for a long life misspent. "You should have thought of that before " has an ungracious ring about it.

XI

THE ACCEPTANCE OF SUFFERING

FATHER GERALD VANN'S latest book, *The Two Trees* (Collins, 2s. 6d.) boldly takes us back to the problem of Suffering. I say " boldly " because much of it was delivered over the wireless, to an audience neither well versed in, nor well attuned to, the Christian philosophy. It is very short, and needs to be read slowly, sipped not gulped, for fear its message should pass us by.

This advantage the author has, that he is preaching to us, and therefore recommending an attitude to us; he wants us to accept suffering in order that suffering may have a meaning for us. If we attend to him, all goes well; we are encouraged, by penitence and sympathy, to associate ourselves with that mysterious current of love by which Christ redeemed and redeems the world. But if we suffer from distractions, we find ourselves asking what suffering means, when it falls on those who do not accept it? It means nothing to them; for whom, then, has their suffering any meaning at all?

Suffering in itself is an evil; it can only be thought of as a good thing because it serves, ultimately, as an expiation of sin; just as a drug which is a poison when we are in good health may become a medicine when we are in the grip of disease. Important, then, surely, that the dispensary of heaven should prescribe it for the right souls; not, this time, the ailing souls, but those who are closest to the spirit of a suffering Redeemer. The mystery ceases, when we are able to reflect that this is a soul which deserves a share in the royal honour of Christ's cross-bearing.

That explains the suffering of the great souls, the great lovers of God. But what of those much more frequent instances, in which the suffering seems to be altogether on a level too heroic for that soul's capacities? Surely we have a right to guess that the acceptance of suffering, even when it is grudgingly given, when there is murmuring at times, has nevertheless a value in God's sight.

Best of all, perhaps, when there is a conscious endeavour to make the best of it, in order to spare the feelings of others. Where a moral agent is concerned, it is always to be hoped that he will also be a moral patient; that he will identify himself, in some degree, with the purpose behind his sufferings. The stiff lip, the Stoical acceptance with which pain is greeted in many lives, have a certain human dignity; it is not difficult to believe that in God's eyes they are at least the raw material of expiation.

XII

PERSEVERANCE

THIS TIME of year, in the hot summer of 1859, died a French *curé* who had spent forty years of life in a small and remote village, the only parish he ever had. The fame of his spirituality was such that twenty thousand pilgrims came to see him in a year, and for the last ten years of his life he spent about seventeen hours a day in the confessional.

That is the story of to-morrow's Saint, John Vianney, the *curé* of Ars. Among all the astonishing features of that record, I count this not least, that he went on and on so. Mostly—it is proverbial—the Saints are short-lived; and for the most part their lives are full of incident; they cross oceans, withstand princes, evangelise a whole countryside. When St. John Vianney died, at seventy-three, you may say he had hardly been out of his parish for forty years; his life had been a routine of sanctity. How did such a man avoid getting into a rut, in the bad sense? You meet, sometimes, old priests who have remained young; Canon Palmer of Ilford, who died the other day, so great and with so little *réclame*, was such a man. But most of us. . . .

Of all graces, clearly, that of perseverance is the most important; *finis coronat opus*. Theologically speaking, that grace is to be found in (say) a life-long criminal who makes a good death-bed repentance. But perseverance as a psychological quality is not the work of a moment. It is faith lasting out over a lifetime. And, to us others, our religion is not the mountain-moving thing it is to the Saints; it feels like a tenuous influence that might be withdrawn almost without our noticing it. Whence does it get the toughness that makes it triumph over the years?

Easy to say, that the mind hardens with age. Our prejudices harden, yes, but not our enthusiasms. Familiarity has staled us, the habit of criticism has grown; we live down a hundred aesthetic and personal preferences. Why is this chance-sown seed perennial?

A grace assuredly, but some human co-efficient it must have in the conscious life of the mind. What are the *signs* of perseverance? Two above all, I suppose; unwelcome, one to sloth, the other to pride. The struggle of Christian life, at any level, is one in which we can never take a holiday. To fall through weakness, to acquiesce, through inadvertence, unimaginativeness, in low ideals—that is pardonable; what we must fear is the temptation to a deliberate let-up. And the other sign is to be always dissatisfied with ourselves. The soul is not yet lost which still wishes it were different.

XIII

THE FEAR OF DEATH

EVERY thoughtful reader of John Wesley's Journal must be struck by the importance it attaches to the triumph of religion over bodily fear. It was precisely their indifference to death, in face of imminent shipwreck, that threw him into a fervid admiration of his Moravian fellow-passengers ; and it was this admiration which forbade him to think of himself as a Christian until a conversion such as theirs should have changed his whole life—a life, already, of the highest purpose, of the strictest discipline. Nothing impressed him (or the world) more about the success of the Methodist preaching than its power to send criminals to the gallows with a conviction, almost amounting to a sense, that they were then and there exchanging this life for a better one. Nothing so disedified him in Ireland as the reluctance of condemned rebels, mere boys, to accept their fate when they had received the last consolations of the Church.

Curiously, you get an exactly contemporary picture, the reverse of the medal. Dr. Johnson, a man of robust views, profoundly Christian in outlook, and much tenderer in his personal religion than in his public attitude seems to have had a fear of death always, except in his last illness. He fidgeted and angrily changed the subject when Boswell tried to pump him about it. Are we to conclude that Johnson was only a half-Christian ? Or that the early Methodists were only enthusiasts, labouring under a delusion which many people would be uncommonly glad to share ?

STIMULI

The contrast must not be so crudely stated. It is a contrast, not between real and notional assent, between *belief* in a religious proposition and casual, unthinking acceptance of it; rather, between two types of mystical approach. There is a mysticism which does not value or recognise faith until it overflows into the feelings; call it, if you will, Moravian. There is a mysticism which distrusts the feelings, and invokes a " naked " faith ready to disregard them and do without them; the less consolation it is given the better; call it, if you will, Quietist. Is it a better thing to go singing to your death like the Moravians or to set your teeth and do your duty, digesting unnamed terrors? Is it possible, and is it important, to adjudge between the two attitudes?

Of all Hugh Benson's books none bites deeper, I think, than *The Coward*. It seems certain that fear is a humiliation, not a sin; that each is required to do his job, not disturbing his neighbour by chattering of tongue or teeth, without skulking or bravado. His private feelings are to be judged only by the God who put them there.

XIV

DESPONDENCY

WE ALL know that there is a theological virtue of hope, and a corresponding sin of despair. But this is within a closely defined area ; we are bidden to hope for, we are not allowed to despair of, the divine mercy. Is there, in general, any reason why Christians should take a roseate view of life ; are they the less Christians if they wring their hands and announce that everything is going from bad to worse ?

A prophet may be sent for the express purpose of destroying the complacency in which a country or a world is sunk; Jeremiah, in modern conditions, would not have remained long outside a concentration camp. But, as a rule, very holy people do impress us, I think, with a feeling of serenity ; they are like grown-ups playing with the children. " All things shall be well," Mother Julian told us, " and all manner of things shall be well." Very holy people are, unfortunately, the exception. If you find yourself walking home from a party in November weather, in troubled times, conscious that you have spread yourself for an hour or more in diagnosing decadence and predicting woe—have you come short of your duty as a Christian ? Or was it fair comment on a matter of public interest ?

Let us remember, in our own defence, that the Christian has more to be depressed about than his neighbours. He shares the head-shakings of the patriot and the moralist, and has an extra grievance of his own about the decline of religion. Let us remember that in such matters, more perhaps than anywhere else, we are at the mercy of temperament. Sanguine or atrabilious, mercurial or saturnine (how expressive it is, the jargon of an older psychology!), we were built that way. We are prone to despondency, and our best efforts to struggle against it will not do more than redress the balance. But all this is in mitigation of the sentence. What of the verdict?

I think it goes against us. Not that I would plead for that artificial cheerfulness which some Christians seem to cultivate as a kind of professional etiquette, a bedside manner. If you have the wrong temperament for it, it wears terribly thin.

No, but to keep your mouth shut when you have got the black dog on your back—surely that is not beyond the compass even of a modest performer. To ease your depression by inflicting it on others ; to pride yourself on being more disillusioned than they ; to wreck, with deliberate *schadenfreude*, the last outposts of their optimism—all that is a kind of intellectual cruelty which, though the pious manuals may not catalogue it among the sins, is something less than Christian.

XV

MORTIFICATION

THE PRACTICE of doing without things you could comfortably afford, or even inflicting discomfort on yourself, is a gesture familiar to most religions. Perhaps the earliest Christians thought of it chiefly in terms of liberty; they would "leave the world," or at any rate stake out for themselves the smallest possible claim on it, in order that their prayers (as St. Paul put it) might not be hindered. That idea of emancipation is preserved in many later ascetic movements; with St. Francis, for example, it is clear that poverty is valued, in great part, as bringing freedom from the trammels of an already burdensome civilisation. There were other considerations, too, which encouraged Christians to live sparingly. As far back as St. Leo you find that giving to the poor is the recognised obverse of denying yourself superfluities; hence the Lenten alms-box, which utters its appeal not less but more insistently to those who are excused from the strict duty of fasting.

But always another element intrudes itself into the picture, that of atonement. The penitent sinner must attest his penitence by identifying himself, not merely in will but in outward fact, with the Divine justice which scourges him. And even where there is no nagging sense of guilt to spur us on, the consciousness that we are members of a sinful race bids us offer expiation, in the form of self-denial, on the general behalf.

The reformed theology, cradled in the controversy over indulgences, looked askance at these works of supererogation. Eager to isolate the merits of the Passion in their unique significance, the Reformers decried, sometimes not without grossness of expression, the ambitions of those who sought to merit heaven by making earth a hell. They could not banish the vocabulary of self-denial. But it became necessary, in disclaiming all human merit, to represent all ascetism as an attempt to toughen your own fibre ; a view which has its own dangers of anthropocentricity.

Partly in reaction from the Lutheran attitude the spiritual writers of the Counter-reformation insisted more vigorously than ever on asceticism as a means of personal holiness. A disproportionate emphasis was given, sometimes, to the heroic mortifications of the Saints. Denying yourself, to the utmost, the use of creatures was represented as if it constituted, instead of paving the way for, a perfect form of life.

In our own day, a fresh reaction has set in ; and you find a tendency in spiritual writers to claim that the right attitude towards creatures is not one of negation but one of affirmation. This view is elusive enough to demand an article of its own ; at the moment I can only take refuge in the mortification of silence.

XVI

THE APOCALYPSE

FEW OF us can lay down the last book of the Bible without a sense of frustration. We have the instinct, or perhaps have accepted the tradition, that the whole thing is a puzzle which would yield up its secret if we could only find out the right clue. And yet, if you try to demonstrate that all these prophecies were fulfilled in the first century, you are reduced to desperate shifts of exegesis. If you hold that some or most of them still remain to be fulfilled, you do violence to your author, whose sense of urgency is manifest, and at the same time you involve yourself in disappointment.

A dangerous itch in our natures would prompt us to identify the Four Horsemen or the Mark of the Beast with contemporary happenings. Religious history is disfigured, century after century, with the scars of that fruitless spiritual conflict. From Abbot Joachim to Edward Irving, the line of prophets has never failed, and has never succeeded. That a set of men, undoubtedly moved by an earnest spiritual purpose, should be impressed by the lapse of exactly 1,260 years between the publication of Justinian's Digest and the execution of Louis XVI, is a tragi-comedy of the human intellect. But how real, how actual, it seemed at the time!

Warned by the fate of such theorists—not a few of them lost their reason over it—we decide to take the part of prudence ; the book is sealed (we tell ourselves) and may remain so for centuries. But if so, what warning, and indeed what meaning, have the thunders of Patmos for us and our contemporaries ?

STIMULI

The dilemma seems to indicate (saving the better judgment of the Church) that we have been too hasty in our assumptions. We have taken it for granted that the Apocalypse is a full, literal blue-print of the Last Judgment and of the signs which will precede it. The message is clouded with imagery; nobody really expects the appearance, now or at a later stage in history, of locusts in breast-plates. Nobody can tell us how deep that uncertainty penetrates into the substance of the story; it is a dream, and has the confused time-sequence, the blurred edges of a dream. Certain assurances emerge unmistakably. That a God reigns; that calamities are sent by him, and with a purpose; that a steady protest against the wrongs of earth goes up in his presence, that our patience must be unlimited, our faith equal to any test—all this it is well to remember, not only in the last days, but in those frequent dress-rehearsals which precede them.

XVII

PRAYING ABOUT THE WEATHER

THE THREE Rogation Days, which come at the beginning of this week, have suffered in modern times from neglect. They are not, it would seem, the survival of any pagan festival; they began in the fifth century, on the occasion of an earthquake in Burgundy. Our ancestors celebrated them by fasting and holding outdoor processions, perhaps less with an eye to possible earthquakes than to annual uncertainty about the prospects of the harvest. Even in country parts they survived the Reformation only in the form of a parochial ceremony known as " beating the bounds "; all mention of earthquakes had disappeared from the Litany, and there was no demand for prayers about the weather in urban districts, more and more industrialised.

To-day, with England going agricultural again, the revival of such devotions would perhaps be a timely step. Unfortunately, although we still give thanks for the harvest, we feel some delicacy about praying for its success. Can we, after all, seek to interfere by our petitions with the distribution of rain and sunshine, without demanding a major miracle ? If anything is prearranged without reference to us (and without much reference, farmers would tell you, to our convenience), surely the depressions over Iceland are.

This delicacy, however, depends on a scruple. We doubt the propriety of asking God to arrange the weather for our benefit on account of the scale of the thing. But in fact the same principle is involved, whether we ask God for small mercies or great ; and (at least where temporal mercies are concerned) we are always asking, when we do so, to have a finger in the Providential ordering of the world. If we pray for a sick child, the virulence of the germ and the constitution of the child are constant factors, just as much as the heavy depression over Iceland. In either case, it seems foolish to try to influence God's decision, when *ex hypothesi* his mind is already made up on the subject— we come, surely, too late. It is not so in reality, because God is outside time, and the prayers we offer are, to him, simultaneous with the ordering of creation. The Christian belief is that, foreseeing our prayers (if you like to put it so), God allows them to have some influence, though we cannot tell how large an influence, on his ordering of creation, sun, rain, and wind thrown in. The children must have their garden.

To be sure, we may hesitate to pray for the abnormal, for snow in August or a heat wave in January. We may make reserves when we pray for *our personal* weather, sunshine for our garden party or rain for our fishing holiday. But to pray, when April is dry or June a deluge, for the restoration of normal conditions is neither to pray for a miracle nor to pray against the interests of the farmer next door. If you believe in praying for temporal blessings at all, you need have no scruple about the Rogation Days.

XVIII

WORLDLINESS

YEARLY on Septuagesima Sunday, with a familiarity that has blunted the edge of astonishment, the Churchgoer is warned by the epistle against the danger of relapsing into idolatry. True, other and more real dangers seem to be indicated—murmuring, for example, against which few of us are proof. But anyone who takes the care to follow up the context will see that idolatry is the real subject. The Corinthians have asked how far it is safe to go in conforming, externally, to the social customs of their heathen neighbours, when these have theological implications. St. Paul replies that we must be on our guard, we are all weaker than we know. He himself subdues his bodily appetites for fear that he, an apostle, should be disqualified in the race for salvation. The Israelites in the wilderness, though " baptised " in the Red Sea and houselled (as it were) from the manna and the Rock, fell back into idolatry nevertheless; and why not the Corinthians ?

The modern Churchgoer does not add so readily, " And why not me? " His temptation, he feels, is not towards polytheism. For him, meat offered to idols would have no special lure. . . . Exactly, nor had meat offered to idols any lure, *as such*, for the Corinthians. No reason to think it was particularly appetising. They wanted to be allowed to eat the sacrificial food, so as not to look any different from their neighbours ; so as not to win the reputation of killjoys, wet blankets at the feast ; so as not to appear censorious. Are the withers of the modern Churchgoer still unwrung? If so, he has a very well or a very ill-ordered conscience. What St. Paul is really frightened of, in the attitude of his converts, is an approach to worldliness.

Worldliness? It has a Victorian ring about it; but only because we are fact-shy nowadays; the thing goes on as merrily as ever. Worldliness is not, in the last analysis, love of possessions, or the habit of courting great personages. It is simply the weakness of fibre which makes us take our standards from the society round us. If we do not want to eat meat sacrificed to idols that is because, in England at any rate, it is not done. If it were the thing, we should want to do it. And everybody, however high or low in the temporal or in the spiritual scale, has a " world "; has a set of acquaintance who are capital fellows and all that but—for him to fall in with their habits, out of human respect, is to fall. We all know it; but few of us will deny that we need, sometimes, to be reminded of it.

XIX

THE GREAT WEEDING

I HAVE always held, St. Augustine notwithstanding, that the parable of the tares refers primarily to scandals within the Church; ill lives lived and false standards upheld by alleged Christians. But evidently it applies also to scandals in the world generally; to plausible rogues who get away with it, plausible philosophies that gain currency, through the chronic inability of nearly everybody to distinguish wheat from tares. The error will last for a time, our time perhaps, but not for ever. Sooner or later there will be a show-down.

In the parable, it is a harvest, accompanied by a delayed process of weeding. The offending elements, now easily distinguished, are tied up in bundles (for the persecutors of the truth make strange bed-fellows) to be burned. Why is it that our modern conceptions of that appalling bonfire lack the medieval gusto? Is it less faith, more charity on our part? Or is it that we have come to think of the false philosopher as the victim, rather than the author, of his philosophy?

Well, let it be a bonfire of things, not persons; of those seductive illusions through which, always *sub specie boni*, men commit hideous wrongs and cruelties. The ultimate victory of truth—to that at least we may look forward with gusto, so long half-tempted to lose heart.

More and more it is possible to define the modern issue as truth versus propaganda. And these are hard times for the creedless idealist, who still reverences the values—truth especially—and sees such reverence being bred out of the minds of conditioned masses. What if the longing for truth should leave men's minds ?

For us, in the darkest hour, there remains the confidence that these values, truth, justice and the rest, have an independent existence in Real Life, though not what is ordinarily meant by Real Life. We hold one end of the clue ; and if the other end is not soon found, no need for disheartenment ; therein lies the patience of the saints.

XX

FIGS AND THISTLES

"BY THEIR fruits you shall know them." Every year, just about the time when thistles are becoming a problem to the agriculturist, he hears read out in church our Lord's assurance that you cannot gather figs from them. Our Lord was speaking of false prophets ; did he mean merely that the proof of the pudding is in the eating ? That the false prophet can keep it up for a time but will give himself away in the end ? Merely that ? Or is he telling us that Christian actions proceed, as by a law of nature, from the Christianised mind ; that the Christian character is an organism which produces its fruits naturally, effortlessly, almost unconsciously ?

Which is better, charity (or meekness, or humility) which is the result of a moral struggle in our natures, or charity which gets to work as surely as a float bobs up to the surface of the water, not thinking about it ? There are two sides to the question. We are inclined to criticise the virtue which costs severe effort as somehow unreal, artificial. On the other hand, virtue which is quite unreflecting " has no merit in it," people say, " because it costs nothing." The moralists will range themselves this way and that in the eternal debate. Miss Dorothy Sayers, whose new book, *The Mind of the Maker,* is giving me agreeable headaches at the moment has no doubts about it at all. " To feel sacrifice consciously as self-sacrifice argues a failure in love. . . . The Puritan assumption that all action disagreeable to the doer is *ipso facto* more meritorious than enjoyable action is firmly rooted in this exaggerated valuation set on pride.

... I do not mean that there is no nobility in doing unpleasant things from a sense of duty, but only that there is more nobility in doing them gladly, out of sheer love of the job."

Christian morality aims, I think, at making a synthesis of the two opposed attitudes. It should transcend both the instinctive generosity of the good-natured man, who throws his money about among the poor as unreflectingly as he puts it on horses, and the laborious efforts of his meaner neighbour, who by a moral *tour de force* manages to part with sixpence, consoling himself the while with copy-book maxims. Its tendency is to create (not without acts of generosity which go against the grain) a generous character which responds to every situation unreflectively, almost automatically, in the right way. Its tendency, but not its aim ; its aim is a closer union with the Person of Christ, from which this generosity flows as a kind of second nature—a redeemed nature. We are wrong if we conceive of our Lord's life as an example we are to follow by cold-blooded imitation *for imitation's sake,* our own nature unaltered the while. He is the tree into which we must be grafted, more and more, until we can produce, not by effort but naturally, its fruits.

XXI

MACHINES AND MEN

RECENTLY the Press recorded the invention of a calculating machine, so ingeniously contrived that it had worked out a sum which had defied, for centuries, human assiduity. They called it a " brain ", and managed to suggest, without saying, that we would soon be producing a race of earth-born men. A scientist, doubtless with tongue in cheek, looked forward to the day when sonnets would be produced by machinery ; only we must not expect to enjoy the sonnets, because they would be such as only the other machines would fully appreciate.

It was such an experience as lifts up the heart, because it reminds you of the obvious but enormously significant fact that man is not a calculating machine ; he is something more. That a metrically perfect sonnet should be produced by machinery is, I suppose, abstractly possible ; and you can imagine the critics detecting some kind of poetic quality in it, for words have an uncanny trick of stirring us by mere force of association. But obviously we are no further on the way to producing a machine which would be affected, pleasurably or otherwise, by a sonnet, its own or another's. We are not in sight of the synthetic Wordsworth until we have endowed a machine with sensitivity, which is a different thing from mathematical calculation ; different not in degree but in kind.

Not that sensitivity, any more than the power of calculation, is man's true definition. I do not know that it would be impossible so to condition a dog that it would react in one way to Sir Philip Sydney, in another to Keats ; nor would we be certain that its experiences differed from our own, for who can analyse the thrill which poetry gives him ? What the dog cannot do any more than the machine, as far as we can either know or guess, is to dissociate itself from its own moment of appreciation ; it cannot become the object of its own thought. Not counting, not aesthetic appreciation, assures us of the perilous position in which we stand ; we have souls.

XXII

IDLENESS

A CORRESPONDENT has asked me to write about idleness. Extraordinary that so little should be written about it, that so few sermons are preached on it. After all, it is responsible for most of our sins of omission ; and how heavily they will weigh on our record ! The reason is, perhaps, that in a given case we can always plead there is no great harm done—to write that letter to-morrow, not to-day, to read one more chapter before I go to bed, can it make much difference ? We English have developed a pose of elegant leisure ; working hours, shopping hours began later with us than with our neighbours ; there was more standing about and leaning against ladders. Now, experts are uncomfortably reckoning out what chances of victory we are throwing away in terms of man-hours. We are beginning to realise that it mounts up. So idleness mounts up in the course of a lifetime.

Sloth is one of the Seven Capital Sins. They are called so, not as being worse than other sins, but as being the fountain-heads from which other sins spring. The others foam down in torrents ; sloth broadens out into an oily morass. We think of sloth in terms of the body ; it suggests love of bed, reluctance to take exercise ; in childhood this was the lesson chiefly rubbed in. But I suspect that the physical inertia which makes it hard to leave one's bed or one's chair, the shrinking from bodily exertion, is enormously a matter of physical make-up, and will be lightly judged. But it *will* be judged ; at this moment, part of the British war effort is the effort Britons make to leave their beds.

STIMULI

Mental sloth is much more insidious, harder to define. Who shall tell us whether this or that duty comes first? Yet choosing the less important of two duties and doing it first is one of the commonest ways of idling. To read such and such a book may be idling for one man; it may be idling for another to leave it unread; it all depends on your state of life. Above all who shall tell us, without bias, how much relaxation really conduces to the efficiency of our lives? Circumstances impose a full programme on some of us; the rest will do well (now, at any rate) to be strict and honest with themselves. An unbraced mind can be a very feeble instrument.

Even more insidious is that spiritual sloth which the Middle Ages called *accidie*; it is significant that we have no name for it. It means that you give up trying; sit with folded hands and wait for things to happen. To live by and for an ideal means constant, hardly perceived spiritual strain; to shirk that strain is *accidie*. Wars can be lost by the loss of the inspiration which should come from a just cause. It is to be feared that many of us lose, in the same way, or nearly lose, the battle of life.

XXIII

GOOD SHEPHERD SUNDAY

GOOD SHEPHERD SUNDAY confronts us, epistle and gospel, with the most gracious and not the least significant of Christian metaphors. Our Lord said, "I am the good Shepherd"; He also said to Peter, "Feed my sheep." Some of his titles he will, others he will not, share with his own human agents. He, no one else, is the Way and the Door, yet Peter shall have the keys. He, no one else is the Truth; but if we thought he only was the Light, we were wrong; his apostles, too, are the light of the world. So here; he, no one else, is the Life and the Bread of Life, but he is not the only Shepherd. There are others, his deputies.

Can we lay down a principle which resolves these antinomies? Surely it means that wherever he claims to be the source of grace, he holds a unique position; where he claims to be the vehicle through which it comes to us, to release and to canalise its activity, there he does not scruple to take human beings into his partnership. To be the Way, the Door, is a privilege of the Divine-human Mediator; to unlock the door, make it available only to those who are in suitable dispositions, is an office that can be shared (albeit with trembling) by our fellow-men. There can be no other Truth; but the Light which flows from it can be reflected, can shine from a hundred facets. There can be no other Life; but others, under his allegiance, can distribute the Food which nourishes that Life. There will always be those who cry out in alarm at the suggestion that any human intermediary can come between the soul and its Redeemer; let them meditate on this paragraph.

Curiously, the word "pastor" has been accepted by almost every denomination as a ministerial title. It conveys the sense of a terrifying responsibility; he who would be a good shepherd must be ready to suffer, die if necessary, on behalf of the sheep. Failure at that test convicts you of being a "hireling"; of having taken over the shepherd's duty from some hidden motive of self-love. We have seen what is the reward on earth of pastoral fidelity; in Poland, in Jugoslavia, and now in Norway. Can we hope that, when things are tidied up again, the different Christianities will have learned to understand one another better, as the result of a common persecution? It has not always been so in the history of the Church. But at least we shall be less surprised at human representatives sharing in our Lord's action, when we have seen them called upon to share in his Passion.

XXIV

THE HELPING HAND

IT IS a principle of religion which we all recognise, even when we are a poor advertisement for it, that the Christian should do as he would be done by. We are perhaps less familiar with the notion, which is nevertheless worth thought, that a Christian ought to be done by as he would do.

I mean this, that when people are for doing us some small kindness, it is our first heathen instinct to say, " Oh, no, thanks, don't bother." We believe, as we say it, that we are saving the other person trouble. Actually, we are indulging our own pride. Who does not know the embarrassment of wondering whether he dare offer to help a friend on with his overcoat, when the friend has reached a certain point in age, perhaps in corpulency ? Will the offer be well received or indignantly refused ? On the same principle, when we are in difficulties ourselves, trivial or serious, the offer of help from a friend immediately tempts us to say no. We cannot put ourselves under an obligation like that. . . .

There is some right on our side. Few things are more unlovely than the attitude of the beggar who has really lost all sense of proper pride ; who cringes to his benefactor, or alternatively accepts his good offices as if unconscious that any obligation has been incurred. We are right to fear, when things go badly with us and help is forthcoming, the danger of a pauperisation of our nature. But it lies with us to see that we are not precipitated into that extreme ; what of the other extreme ? Will not a moment's reflection often convince us that our " No, thank you " is dictated by a morbid spirit of independence? That proper pride has transgressed its true frontier, and degenerated into surliness?

If it is a Christian habit to accept benefits, as well as to confer them, what Scripture text (I shall be asked) can I adduce in proof of it? The objection, if it is made, comes from one who cannot see the wood for the trees. My text is the Incarnation. Almighty God, living on earth as Man, was content to be nursed by a human Mother, to let good women minister to him, to be ferried by friendly boatmen over waves on which he could walk dry-shod, when he chose. That text should be glaring enough to reconcile us all to constant dependence on one another. Lest it should be overlooked, he gave a final emphasis to it by accepting a drink of wine in the article of death.

War or post-War, the years that lie ahead are going to hit us all, but some harder than others. Please God, we shall not forget the duty of giving a helping hand; we are more likely to forget the duty of taking it. So, the finest natures among us will be in danger of spoiling their own temper; by an attitude which may be good Stoicism, but is bad Christianity.

XXV

THE LAST WAR BUT ONE

NOVEMBER the Eleventh has long been a day of remembrance, rather than of rejoicing. History continued its cynical progress, and left us more conscious of a sacrifice than of a deliverance. To-day, for the first time we celebrate Martinmas no longer as recalling " the end of the war." A fresh melancholy supervenes, as we reflect that our old mood of November melancholy is now "dated."

So, in our private griefs, a fresh ache comes with the healing of the scar. We reproach ourselves with disloyalty because memory weakens. Year by year, the poppies have been a reminder to us; now we are conscious that the poppy, after all, is a symbol of forgetfulness. Do we forget the significance of the old " Armistice Day "? And shall we be forgiven it, if we forget?

Autumn is strewn with these leaves of half-cherished commemoration. October the 21st is sacred to Trafalgar, October the 25th to Balaclava and more distantly to Agincourt. By now, 1854 seems almost as distant as 1805, or even as 1415.

Must 1918 be swept away on to the same bonfire of dead yesterdays? We are the more apprehensive of such a threat, because our younger contemporaries seem, compared with ourselves, impatient of the past. History is apt to be dismissed by the modern age, as " Queen Anne." Is the love of the past itself a thing of the past? Must the dead, in that cruel sense, bury their dead?

Are they a part of *reality*, the events, however recent, that are gone? A philosophy which confines reality to the experience that is with us at the moment of speaking involves serious difficulties. But does the past *live*? There was a great moment at which the German Empire was defeated; is that moment still part of reality? Or does it live only in certain human memories, and, as those memories fade, will it sink into mere nothingness? Do not tell us that the past continues in being because, only because it has contributed to the present; that would evoke too poignant memories of the War that was to end war. Must it be written down with the snows of yesteryear?

Reality, perhaps, belongs to people rather than to things. But what about the people; the people who were alive in 1914, and had become memories by 1918? Have they, outside memory, no existence? The riddle of existence becomes less of a nightmare if we can believe that the souls of the just are in the hand of God. Not distant from us, really, in time, or place, or state; they are in God's hand, which he keeps hidden behind his back, as grown-ups will when they are teasing children.

XXVI

LEAD, KINDLY LIGHT

WHEN Newman wrote what is probably one of the dozen most popular hymns in the language, as far back as 1833, he did not for a moment guess—we have his own word for it—where he was being led ; the " distant scene " was unimaginable to him. One step was enough ; but the process was in fact to culminate on October 9th, 1845, when he found his Canossa at Littlemore. His fellow countrymen, most of them quite otherwise minded, have yielded to the magic of his hymn, and read, not dry-eyed, the story of his conversion.

Essentially, what he gave up was not such and such a belief or disbelief, but the privilege of " choosing and seeing his path." That is why his conversion ranks with those of St. Paul, St. Augustine, Pascal, and a few others as a great historical moment. One of the world's choice souls was overcoming hesitation and renouncing the management of its own destiny.

Notoriously, it is the gift of great poets to universalise ; a phrase flashes out from their writings which seems to fit everyone's private griefs. You need not be exactly in Aeneas's shoes to console yourself with Virgil's " These will be happy memories one day " ; you need not be exactly in Othello's shoes, to murmur " Oh now for ever farewell, the tranquil mind."

Newman's three stanzas have the same magic ; you may be nothing of a theologian, you may be (or think you are) in no need of fresh intellectual illumination, and yet the

words come straight home. When Newman wrote " the
night is dark," he was thinking about controversial issues ;
about the dawn of Liberalism and the suppression of the
Irish bishoprics. The preoccupations of your own mind
may be far less polemical, far more personal ; but you are
in a bad way if you do not feel the need of *some* kindly
Light for your guidance.

The readiness to keep his eyes blindfolded, to follow
the Divine call wherever it might lead him, was not, for
Newman, the caprice of a moment; it was the inspiration
of a long, and in some ways a difficult life. It is an attitude
God loves to find in the soul ; must (humanly speaking)
find in a soul if he is to do anything with it. His " sacrament of the present moment," keeping all your mind concentrated on the thing you ought to be doing here and now,
because it is his will, blindfolding yourself to what the
future has in store, never wasting yourself on day-dreams
or unnecessary alarms—that is the key-attitude of Christian
resignation. And it will never be more justly phrased than
it was, by a great and sensitive soul, a hundred years ago.

XXVII

RECESSIONAL

OUR LORD only once inculcates the duty of thanksgiving, and that indirectly, when he asks what has happened to the nine lepers who did not come back. Only once does he express gratitude himself, in John xi. 41—in Matthew xi. 25 the word should be " praise." St. Paul insists on this duty almost wearisomely ; there are some forty references to it in his epistles, and in several of them he seems to drag it in gratuitously. Meanwhile, our Lord is described several times by the Evangelists as giving thanks, but only at the Last Supper, his Eucharist and at the miracle of the Loaves which foreshadowed and typified it.

Is it possible that he deliberately concentrated attention upon the liturgical expression of gratitude ; as if gratitude were a business not to be gone about lightheartedly ? As if we were not likely, left to ourselves, to make a success of it ?

Gratitude, in so far as it is really felt, conveys a sense of inferiority ; that is where the shoe pinches. In our human relations that does not matter very much because we look forward vaguely to some later opportunity of repaying the favour we have received ; we will get quits, one day, with our benefactor. But common sense assures us that there is no paying off scores with a Benefactor who is Divine. We can give him nothing but what is already his own ; do nothing for him but what he himself enables us to do.

There can be no payment, then, but a kind of token payment ; and in so far as we let our minds dwell on the fact of a boon granted, they will close on the unpalatable thought that we are debtors still.

This is hard enough in our private affairs ; doubly hard when we are called upon to give thanks for a great national deliverance. To tell God that we owe the victory entirely to him feels as if we were casting aspersions on the competence of our own statesmen or our own generals. We know, of course, that such contrasts are unreal, but the feeling is there. Worse still, to tell God that we did not deserve the victory suggests to us that the other side did ; are we going to admit that our English folk—so kindly in general, whatever their faults may be—are just as bad as the Germans ? Once more, we know that that is not the point ; that the Germans deserved to lose does not mean that we deserved to win. But the feeling is there.

All the more grateful should we be, amidst these embarrassments, for having a liturgical means of approach which leaves the thanksgiving in other Hands than ours a veritable Eucharist.

XXVIII

THE INNOCENT SUFFERER

THERE has been much undeserved suffering in the world these last six years; what optimist doubts that there is much undeserved suffering at this moment? Is it allowable to draw breath in the moment of triumph and commiserate the wronged, on this Easter-tide Sunday when the liturgy seems to plunge back into Holy Week? I am thinking especially of the Epistle, the last five verses of 1 Peter ii.

We forget that the words were expressly written for the benefit of slaves. Cappadocia was one of the countries St. Peter addressed, and Cappadocian slaves were notoriously tough and stupid. They must often have suffered for no fault of their own; he tries to make them see that it doesn't matter what people think; the only thing that matters is what God thinks. It would be difficult for them, stupid people, to appreciate that without a pattern written out large, like the heading of a copy-book. They have such a pattern, the evening of Maundy Thursday.

St. Peter knows what he is talking about; he was there. He knew something about slaves, because he had spent one unforgettable evening in the servants' hall. You do not forget the evening on which you have denied your Master. Our Lord " did no wrong," yet he was taunted and buffeted; he was taunted and buffeted, yet he "spoke no evil in return, suffered, and did not threaten vengeance." St. Peter had only to shut his eyes for that picture to come back to him.

And he, what had he been doing all the time? Lying to

save his skin, cursing indignantly over a charge that was
perfectly true. In Gethsemane, he had been guilty of the
unpardoned sin—interfering with the police in the performance of their duty. He escaped, because our Lord said
" If I am the man you are looking for, let these others go
free." It comes back to him, as he sits in the catacombs
writing to his Cappadocian friends, so ready with the
defence " It was him, not me, done it."

That attitude of our Lord's was but a symbol of what he
was in fact doing when he suffered—taking upon himself
the punishment of our sins, due from us in eternity. But
it was also a pattern, for Cappadocians and others. " I will
smite the shepherd, and the sheep shall be scattered," our
Lord quoted on that last night ; inevitably, at moments of
panic and crisis, his pattern of unselfishness is forgotten.
" Now " adds the Apostle, " you have been brought back
to him, your shepherd " ; in peace time, we fall back on
the heavy task of digesting our wrongs.

XXIX

FORGIVENESS AND FORGIVINGNESS

PUNISHMENT, according to the traditional account of it, involves three elements : it is retributive, corrective, deterrent. It should restore a balance where wrong has been done ; if it is accepted in the right spirit it improves the character of the offender ; at worst, it discourages others from imitating him. Those philosophers who would leave out the first consideration undermine the whole morality of punishment. (Why, for example, do we distinguish between murder and homicide ?) Where Divine punishments are concerned, that is the whole account of the matter. Human justice, administered by fallible and imperfect creatures, is liable to be influenced by a disturbing factor—that of vindictiveness.

We are vindictive, not necessarily when we impose a heavy penalty on the wrongdoer, but when we rejoice in imposing it. The deplorable thing is not strictness of temper, but savagery of motive. In the ordinary procedure of the courts, the question of revenge seldom arises ; though even here a local jury, or a jury representing the interests of some special class, may fail in its duty to be impartial. But where the plaintiff has also to be the judge—and this is the situation when a war terminates in unconditional surrender—the case is otherwise. The administration of justice calls, then, for a deliberate effort of self-control before the victor can take upon himself, without misgiving, the awful role of judge and executioner.

The question is often asked, and can be legitimately asked, Is it possible to punish a whole country ? But we are not concerned here with that question, nor to consider the kind or the amount of punishment due in any individual case. Granted that our present enemies have deserved a communal penalty, granted that it will be our business, not merely to secure the world against future aggression but to exact retribution for crimes committed in the past, we may still err by approaching that business in the wrong spirit. Avoid, by all means, the insincere approach of the legendary school-master, " This hurts me more than it hurts you." But punish the offender because it has got to be done, not because your fingers are itching to do it. The beatings which impressed us at school were administered dispassionately, not in hot blood.

The ordinary citizen will have little say in what happens after the armistice. But I think we have individually a duty not to encourage ourselves or other people in the vindictive spirit. We may hold that forgiveness, freely granted to our present enemies, would be a betrayal of trust and a perversion of justice. But there is still a virtue in *forgivingness*; in excluding the voice of mere passion from the council-chamber of the heart.

XXX

SWORDS AND PLOUGHSHARES

THE INSTITUTION of Farm Sunday, which is only the rehabilitation of Rogation Sunday, should be a matter of rejoicing to town-dwellers. It is not to be supposed, that in emphasising the importance of agriculture in a religious setting, Christians are making a division between town and country, as if towns were all haunts of vice, and villages were all homes of sabbath peace. The Prince of Darkness is a gentleman, and not seldom takes his week-end in the country. Nor are we setting up agriculture against industry, the man against the machine.

On Farm Sunday we should think not only of farmers and farm labourers, but of the factories where they make ploughs and drills and harrows ; of the millers, too, and the bakers, and all who work to prepare food for us. The contrast we indicate is a different one, more directly concerned with the conditions of the moment.

At the present moment, all the industries which are not concerned with the production of food have gone over to war-time activities ; they are subserving the purposes of destruction. We do not cast a slur on the heroism of our armed forces when we point out that they are a body of men commissioned to destroy. Even when they are not destroying human lives, they are destroying human wealth. They do so fully authorised, for a purpose ultimately beneficent, with supreme courage—there is no loophole for criticising them. But their work is in itself a work of *unmaking*. Whereas the farmer and his allies, sheltered and inconspicuous, are still at their old trade of bringing food out of the earth; theirs is a work of *making*. The soldier creates cosmos through chaos; the farmer cosmos out of chaos.

For, indeed, in all his activities, if he will view them with humility, Man is only a secondary cause, furthering the work of God. The farmer is not likely to forget this, indebted as he is to uncharted processes of rain and sunshine for his results. The soldier is in more danger of forgetting whose uniform, ultimately, he wears; but he, too, is only a secondary cause. A nation in arms must, with a hideous responsibility, regard itself as the minister of Divine Justice against those who have defied it; there is no excuse, otherwise, for man killing man. The soldier abets and reflects God's work of judgment; the farmer abets and reflects God's work of creation. There is no difficulty in seeing which has inherited the more gracious office.

Let Farm Sunday, then, stand as witness to us, in days when we are in danger of forgetting it, that making not unmaking, life, not death, is the true watchword of the universe.

Nihil Obstat: Eduardus Mahoney, S.T.D.
Censor Deputatus

Imprimatur: E. Morrogh Bernard
Vic. Gen.

Westmonasterii, Die 22a Januarii, 1951